MW01273507

NOW START WITH WHO

Serving Is The New Selling

JON MORRISON

DEEZIA
PUBLISHING

Now Start With Who: Serving Is The New Selling

Published By: Deezia Press

Vancouver, B.C.

©2020 by Jon Morrison

All rights reserved. No part of this publication may be reproduced, stored in a retrieval system, or transmitted by any means without prior written consent of the author.

ISBN-13: 9798624077942

Praise For Now Start With Who

"*Now Start With Who* is a timely reminder that our businesses exist to make our customers' lives better."

Chip Wilson, Founder of *lululemon* and author of *Little Black Stretchy Pants*

"Jon's passion for serving people is a breath of fresh air in the business world. His message will encourage your heart, renew your passion and help your team get clear on its mission to help customers."

Trevor Throness, CEO of *Getting People Right* & Author of *"The Power of People Skills"*

"Jon Morrison has helped my chiropractic practice and many others get clear on their messaging. I teach chiropractors about marketing and Jon has been a vital aspect of helping my chiropractors get laser-focused on their marketing message."

Dr. Kevin Christie, Author of *Doing It Right: Modern Chiropractic Marketing* & Co-Founder of the *Chiropractor Success Academy*

"Jon Morrison is a master of reducing confusion. His skills and this book will help you declutter your marketing, which will declutter your website, and your business life. Not only will your marketing become simplified, but your customers will buy more often since they aren't confused. I can't recommend him enough."

Dr. Josh Satterlee. Author of *Clinic/Gym Hybrid Secrets: The Revolutionary Method to Maximize Your Chiropractic License, Have The Clinic of Your Dreams, and Live The Life You Desire!*

"Jon Morrison has so eloquently identified that the crux of any business and any relationship, for that matter, is the 'Who.' If we can start with our 'Who,' we will easily be able to identify the corresponding 'Why, What and How.' This is such a critical book for all organizational leaders!"

Tim Dumas, CEO of *Servus Leadership*

Acknowledgements

When you are trying to lead two companies and a family with three girls under six, writing a book is a team effort.

I'd like to take a few moments to thank the people who were part of my team in publishing this book.

To Those Who Guided My Thinking

You could say that it takes as much work to think of something important as it does to make sure those ideas actually get passed on. I'm thankful for the thought leaders who served as a catalyst for the ideas found in this book.

I'm thankful for Don Miller and the team he has put together at StoryBrand. For over twenty years, Don has been one of my favourite authors. For the last five years, I have used the Story-Brand framework to help businesses worldwide create a clear marketing message. Much of this thinking helped shape my passion for my customer-centric "Start With Who" framework. I am thankful to the StoryBrand community who has modelled excellence and professionalism to grow the Get Clear brand.

I am also in debt to thinkers like Seth Godin, Jon Acuff, and Simon Sinek. They may never know the impact they have made on my thinking.

I'm grateful for the programs of Dan Martell (*Growth Accelerator*), Dan Sullivan (*Strategic Coach*), and Nicky Billou (*eCircle Academy*). You have inspired me to write a book that could impact people and grow my own thought leadership. I love your determination to provide water bottles to thirsty entrepreneurs as they learn to thrive in the marathon of business.

To The Colleagues Who Encouraged And Empowered Me To Write

An exhortation is a word of encouragement or critique to make someone or something better. This book and I received a great deal of exhortation along the way.

I thank Marius Deezia, for helping me shape and then reshape and then reshape once more the *Now Start With Who* outline. His passion for empowering authors and showing patience with me was a sign of his excellent character. I hope many more aspiring authors discover his work and create literature with the help of Deezia Publishing.

I am grateful to my team at Get Clear. They show up every day and work hard to make our clients' lives better. My colleagues have freed up my time, allowing me to put in the hours to write a book (and still be able to feed my family.

Lisa Pike has been a huge gift as an editor. It is a pleasure to work with her on the Get Clear team. While it is usually our clients who benefit from her work, this time I was the benefactor. Jack Ainley, also an editor, is a true professional. His recommendations and additions made these pages a much more enjoyable read. He deserves more credit than he will ever get.

I am grateful for my chiropractor clients, whose partnership has opened up many doors for me. Because of their entrepreneurial spirit, I've been able to try new ideas and explore new opportunities in online marketing. As I was writing this book, I was thinking about the conversations I have had with them over the years. They've opened up their lives and their businesses to me, creating partnerships that have led to lifelong friendships. As you'll see in the coming pages, I have stumbled into helping these awesome people. With years of hindsight now, I clearly see that everything happens for a reason. I'm glad they've welcomed me into their community.

To Those Who Inspire Me

I dedicate this book to my three amazing daughters; Abigail, Grace and Lucy.

They make life fun and meaningful. They inspire me to become a better dad, husband, and human being. I'm thankful for their reminder each day about what is most important in life.

For my wife, Hayley, I am immensely thankful. I have appreciated Hayley's feedback throughout the writing process. No doubt, the burden of writing this book was felt hardest by her. With three busy kids and a home to manage, she had to pick up the slack as I would often have to sneak away to get writing done (AM and PM and AM all over again). This excludes the time I'd be working through an idea, staring into space and completely ignoring anything that was going around me.

I'm thankful to Jesus, my Leader. I'm grateful he can use my love of words to help others. For the comfort, health, shelter, provision, and the second chance at a career that puts food on the table for my family and others, I will always be grateful.

For you, the reader, I'm thankful that you still value books and ideas enough to devote some of your precious time and attention to them. You are my kind of people. That being said, it's time to start, *Now Start With Who*.

Contents

ONE

Introduction: It's All About People

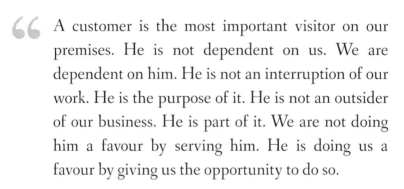

A customer is the most important visitor on our premises. He is not dependent on us. We are dependent on him. He is not an interruption of our work. He is the purpose of it. He is not an outsider of our business. He is part of it. We are not doing him a favour by serving him. He is doing us a favour by giving us the opportunity to do so.

- Mahatma Ghandi

The COVID-19 pandemic was the most disruptive force that most of us have ever experienced. We will feel its impact for decades to come.

While the virus brought disastrous setbacks to so many areas of life, COVID-19 launched our world ahead by ten years in so many ways.

For example, we saw giant leaps forward in retail. In 2019, we all knew e-commerce was the future of retail. We just didn't presume that our grandparents would figure out how to shop for our 2020 Christmas presents on Amazon. Most brick and mortar stores scrambled in the Spring of 2020 to get their products online to avoid going out of business. Out of necessity, COVID-19 brought e-commerce to the masses much quicker than we expected.

Those are just a few examples of how society's evolution was catapulted ten years forward by the virus.

What changed for you during the pandemic?

We are all a little different. Your customers certainly changed. How did your business change with them? Many businesses did not survive the pandemic. For many of them, based on how things were going pre-COVID, shutting down was inevitable. What would've happened at some time in the coming decade, COVID accelerated quickly. Some time ago, these struggling companies lost touch with the one essential element they need to survive and thrive in business today: *A commitment to serve people.*

When they lost that, the writing was on the wall. The COVID-19 crisis delivered it quicker than we thought.

Perhaps your business has lost its commitment to serve people. You and your team could use a fresh vision and inspiration for the customers that will fuel your business for decades to come. This book will reconnect you, your team, and your business to the people you may be missing the most right now: *your cherished customers*.

My hope is that the lessons learned during the pandemic brought you closer to your customers.

My fear is that you may have drifted from them during the disruption.

The One Thing Businesses Must Do

One of the consequences of automating, economizing, and digitizing everything is that we can quickly lose track of why our business exists in the first place.

Every business primarily exists to serve its customers.

While many perks come with having a business (the earning of wages, the trips, the tax write-offs, and company golf tournaments), a business exists to make a customer's life better. Too many business leaders and entrepreneurs have forgotten about how important people are. For many of us, it took a global pandemic to remind us how good it is to have people around - and how much we struggle without them.

Helping people is mission-critical for any company to make money. Reaching more people is critical to sustainable growth.

In this book, we are calling those people your "Who."

Every business has a Who. Your Whos are the people you love to help, that you're good at helping, and they are the people who are happy to pay you well for it. Others have called them your "ideal client," "customer avatar," or a whole host of other names that consultants have come up with over the years.

Again, every business primarily exists to serve its customers. You'll soon see the benefits of re-centering around this idea - putting customers as the focus of what you do. In doing so, you'll reach more of them. We've got a lot of case studies of thriving businesses that have done just that.

It's time to do a check for what is pumping the heart of your business. It's time to rediscover your core conviction for helping people. It's time to Start With Who.

What A Novel Virus Taught Us About How Much We Need People

When I started writing this book near the end of 2019, I had no idea what was coming in 2020. Did anybody see 2020 coming?

- There was a toilet paper shortage
- A lot of people died.
- There was a global pandemic
- Nobody agreed on anything

- Many businesses struggled, some closed and some thrived
- We saw massive social unrest
- We endured another excruciating US election

It's a year full of stories that will be passed on for generations.

Who could forget the scramble for PPE, the refrigerated mobile morgues parked outside of hospitals, and the plexiglass everywhere.

While it was a boom year if you worked for Amazon, owned shares of Tesla, or could quickly pivot to e-commerce, it was one of the most challenging seasons we've all had to go through.

Serving people is mission-critical to the health of any business.

2020 was a truly unique experience because it's something that we, the whole world, experienced together.

Some willingly and some reluctantly, we went into lockdown and isolated. We lost our sports, office culture, restaurants, favorite annual conferences, attending church, being moved by concerts, and going to school.

And we lost our minds sometime between the second and third wave.

We noticed an ache build-up in us. Separated from the events that made life fun, we learned that the true joy in all the usual activities was never the events themselves. What made "going out" meaningful was the people with whom we shared the experience.

Just like with these public events and outings, it's the people that make your business meaningful too.

Events were never about the event itself. It was about the people.

Putting people back at the heart of why you do what you do is the driving principle of *Now Start With Who*. I want to show you how critical it is to have your customers at the core of your business strategy.

Connecting with people wasn't only a problem in 2020. For many of us, it has always been a struggle. It may not be connecting that's the issue. It's connecting with the right people we find such a challenge.

For Those Struggling To Connect With People

It troubles me that most of us go through each day frustrated because we know our best ideas are not getting the attention they deserve.

Why is that happening? We have a people problem.

Our ideas are not connecting with the people that need to hear them.

You may have an amazing idea for a business you want to start. Perhaps it is a service or product you want to add. It could be a cause you want to advance. You may have an organization you want to improve or a new process that will increase efficiencies and profits.

No doubt, what you've got inside of you could help many people. But you don't need to be convinced of that. Other people do.

It would serve everyone best if you find a way to effectively transfer that passion from you to others. Imagine if they could share the excitement you feel. Imagine if they could see things as clearly as you do.

The problem is (and we all know it), they don't.

For Those Struggling To Achieve Their Purpose

The title "Now Start With Who" is intentionally provocative.

We start the book engaging with the ideas of Simon Sinek and the "Start With Why" movement which has emerged to cult level status in the business community.

Sinek wrote an influential book about the importance of finding your "Why" in life. I appreciate this book and its influence on our culture today. It has inspired millions of people to look for purpose and meaning in life and business. The reality is that not everyone who read *Start With Why* is taking the proper steps to achieve it. In fact, they haven't taken any steps at all.

This can be discouraging. To know your Why and not be actively taking the proper steps towards it is to miss the very reason we think we are alive.

In the next chapter, I'll reveal the reasons I see this happening. In the meantime, I will tease out my theory: We don't get our "Why" because we have a Who problem. Put another way, we struggle to achieve our purpose because we can't get people helping us do it. We are missing the people needed to get behind our Why.

Great Whys go unfulfilled because no one else buys into them. Why seekers are missing a strategic element to achieving anything significant, this element will capture the right people's attention and generate a movement when appropriately applied.

Starting With Who provides the strategy to:

- achieve your purpose
- grow a business with your favourite customers
- improve your marketing
- streamline your communication
- clarify your message
- advance your cause
- get the traction your ideas deserve
- increase your satisfaction in life
- achieve your Why

You're about to learn the importance of finding a specific group of people and helping them win in life. You'll learn to diagnose what is causing them pain so that you become the leader they've been looking for. Our goal will be to help you create marketable solutions that improve their lives by helping them overcome the problems holding them back.

When you Start With Who, you make a difference on a micro and macro level. The right product, service, course, or new technology can profoundly change a life. That's micro. When one life changes, a whole family can benefit. When families are better, we see transformation in entire communities. When you see that happen, you've made your mark on this planet. That's the macro change for which many of us aspire.

Any kind of real success in life involves impacting people. There are few significant achievements accomplished in history that didn't involve people.

Human connection is essential to the success of your business.

Human connection is essential to the vitality of your business.

People are not your problem. People are your goal. As we look at reconnecting with customers, we discover just how powerful helping real people can be.

Now let me tell you how a string of lousy dating relationships, a Facebook Group with thousands of chiropractors, and my early days as a Baptist preacher led to the development of why we should Start With Who. It's a principle I'm excited to share with you.

I'm convinced it transforms your life and business.

TWO

You Get Your "Why" When You Start With "Who"

 Look after people, and people will look after you.

– Sam Walton

Too many of our friends, family, members, business colleagues and customers feel like they lack purpose in life. I don't blame them for feeling that way. They've been told since they were young that humanity's existence is meaningless. When you're only one in over 7.5 billion people on the Earth, how do you feel special? If we humans are just one of the zillions of other organisms struggling to live out some kind of existence while inhabiting planet Earth, what's the point? What do you do with the discovery that our planet is just one big molten rock circling a giant star that scientists tell us will blow up or burn out one day?

What do you think it does to someone to hear messages that their existence has no meaning in the big picture? Intelligent people figure out quickly that if life has no meaning in the big picture, neither does it matter in the small one.

If we humans are no different from dirt, grass, or animals, what's the point of trying to make something or do something with our lives? Why spend our finite time at work trying to serve others and make a living?

We've been told this for a long time. It has left many discouraged, and others have given up on life altogether. We have a poverty of purpose in our world today.

Human Beings And Pursuit Of A "Why"

Thankfully, millions of people have rejected the idea that their life is meaningless. Many people have Simon Sinek's work to thank for their new-found sense of purpose. Sinek's message gave a generation of otherwise hopeless people the belief that their life could serve a bigger cause. Sinek calls it a "Why". A Why is the goal that makes you excited to get out of bed each morning. It's the driver that keeps you going; keeps you reaching for a life of significance.

Since the 2009 release of Simon Sinek's *Start With Why*, business leaders, entrepreneurs, entire companies, and organizations of all sizes have scrambled to figure out their "Why." All around the world, they've huddled around board room tables or taken four-day naval-gazing retreats to find their "Why."

Several of my friends confessed to losing sleep trying to figure out their own Why.

The reason they have stressed about it is because discovering your purpose is a powerful milestone in life and business. Knowing your Why, however, doesn't get you across the chasm. It just opens your eyes to a new starting point.

Now the real challenge comes. I fear too many people who get inspired by starting with Why never get to the other side called "Win."

That's what I noticed when researching this book. I talked to colleagues, clients, and other business leaders about their Why. When I asked how they figured it out, they lit up like a Christmas tree. Everyone loves to discuss their Why. If you ever run out of things to say at a business networking event, just drop Simon Sinek's name and you'll have a whole crowd around you in minutes. When I asked businesses how they were *applying* what they learned from Sinek, their countenance changed. They stared at the floor. They shuffled their feet. They tried to change the topic. Suffice it to say; they were ashamed that they weren't where they should be.

Here's what I observed in my survey: Most fans of Simon Sinek and the "Start With Why" approach struggle with applying the material. It turns out that achieving one's Why is no easy endeavor. We all start with the best of intentions. It's just that our follow-through is lacking. Time passes, and we don't get any further ahead, bridging the gap between "Why" and "Win."

There's a reason for this. It took me several years to diagnose the problem and prescribe the solution.

The Chasm

There exists a vast chasm between *knowing* your purpose and *actually achieving it*. How do you know if you're one of the few who figure out the way to bridge the distance between inspiration and transformation?

We are going to learn the process how to go from "This is an inspiring vision for my life and business..." to the thrill of arriving on the other side. I'm calling this a "Win".

Picture two cliffs on each side of a span. On the one side of the cliff there are three giant letters. "W", "H", and "Y". "Why" is the driver for what motivates you to do what you do each day.

On the other side are the letters: "W", "I", "N". "Win" means that you've achieved what you started out to do. You arrived. You crossed the chasm. You finished the journey, accomplishing what you sought out to do.

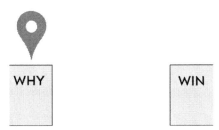

The problem is that far too many people are comfortable on the "Why" side and never leave. They know their Why but years pass and they don't get anywhere closer to the other side. Without the right bridge, they fall into the abyss of obscurity. Then they climb out and try again. But with no bridge built, it's the same result.

With time, those letters "W-H-Y" fade. As discouragement sets in, the Why moves to the other side. By this point, getting to the Why with the Win seems unattainable. This leaves you more discouraged and hopeless than you were before you knew what a Why even was.

Why People Don't Win

Many people don't achieve their Why because the Start With Why approach doesn't adequately equip us to make the jump from inspiration to application.

Let me use one glaring example I resonate with the most. In chapter five of the best-selling book, *Start With Why*, Simon Sinek tells the story of a man named "Brad" who struggled to win the heart of a girl he fancied. In Sinek's account, Brad messed up his first impression with that ever important first date. We know from how Sinek described the date that Brad loved bragging about himself. It's not hard to picture the situation. We've all met someone like this. Brad is the kind of guy who loves talking about his ideas, his dreams, his awards, his job, and anything else he wants to bring attention to in order to reveal how great he is. It's not that he loves talking about those things - it's that he *only* talks about them. Why did Brad struggle on this date and all his other dates? There are a few ideas to consider. Here's how Simon Sinek diagnoses the problem.

On their only date, Sinek recalls how Brad mistakenly only offered this potential suitor *the pure facts about his life*. According to Sinek, Brad mistakenly spoke about his wealth, his fame, and his many exotic experiences as data point. To Sinek, Brad's goal was purely the transformation of information to another. It was about numbers and facts. Sinek argues that if only Brad had offered the compelling "Why" around the information, he would have had more success in winning over the girl. As I read Sinek's advice, I became convinced that the best-selling author and most-viewed TED speaker's suggestion wouldn't work either.

Here is the script proposed by Sinek taken directly from *Start With Why*. This is what Sinek recommends Brad *should have* expressed to the girl on their first date. Note that the information/data is still all there, but Sinek has flowered it up a bit:

 'Do you know what I love about my life?' he starts this time, 'I get to wake up every day to do some-

thing I love. I get to inspire people to do the things that inspire them. It's the most wonderful thing in the world. In fact, the best part is trying to figure out all the different ways I can do that.

It is amazing. And believe it or not, I've been able to make a lot of money from it. I bought a big house and a nice car. I get to meet lots of famous people and I get to be on TV all the time, which is fun because I'm good looking. I'm very lucky that I'm doing something that I love, I've actually been able to do pretty well because of it.'[1]

Sinek's advice is that instead of just flat out saying, "I'm a big deal," Brad should disguise it with some humble bragging. Sinek's goal for Brad is to list how great he is and veil it with statements about beliefs and values (what will be called the "Why").

Here's a better approach for guys like Brad, who can't wait to talk about how great they are on a first date:

Don't do it.

Here's the truth: Other people don't care about how big of a deal you think you are. I know that's tough to hear for some. But it's an insight that will help us make the kind of connections we crave with people.

We shall soon see that what's true in dating is true in business.

One of the reasons we get stuck at "Why" is because we have an overinflated sense of self-importance. We think everyone should be impressed by our "Why". But they're not. We discuss the reasons for this in detail later.

Here's a thought for impressing people: What if Brad didn't start by talking about Brad at all? What if Brad asked questions instead of offering his credentials? Brad would have a lot more success on dates if he took a genuine interest in the person sitting across from him, rather than the *Humble-Brag-With-My-Why* technique.

To anyone like Brad, who have honest intentions to achieve something important but haven't been able to get others to buy-in, I offer a better way. I know it because I've lived it.

I Was Brad. Then I Learned There's A Better Way

I can hear a disaster like Brad's and Sinek's dating strategy like an oncoming freight train. For years, friends and family watched me try to find love like one observes an auto accident - you witness it happening, you cringe, and yet you can't stop staring. Looking back, I see the glaring flaw in my approach to dating. Let me lay out my old methodology for you. You'll soon see why it never worked.

First, I would meet a nice girl and take her out for coffee—nothing out of line so far, I'd say.

Next, I would work hard to impress the date by dropping my many "Whys" that I've accumulated in my life. I was passionate about my many Whys for sure. Like:

- *Why* I love sports ("I like to stay active. That reminds me, did you know I played competitive hockey growing up?")
- *Why* I'm important ("Let me tell you about some sort-of-famous people I've met...")
- *Why* I'm interesting ("I've traveled to some very exotic places...")
- *Why* I'm one of the good guys ("Here are some social issues I'm passionate about because it's cool to be in to things like this these days...")

Do you see a flaw in this approach to winning someone's affections?

You could almost hear my poor dates thinking out loud, "He is passionate for sure. He is passionate *about himself*." The girls would likely return to their friends and say,

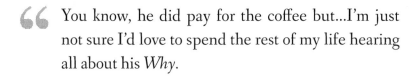 You know, he did pay for the coffee but...I'm just not sure I'd love to spend the rest of my life hearing all about his *Why*.

My Strategy That Failed Miserably

With wisdom and enough hindsight, I see that endlessly talking about my "Why" led to a string of broken relationships. It was always about me. That approach didn't work. Helping others not make the same mistake is what inspired this book. After reading chapter five of *Start With Why*, I had a burning passion for challenging Simon Sinek's ideas and offering an alternative way forward for his fans. I thought maybe sharing my experience could help someone avoid the pain I went through.

Those conversations ended up as the book you are holding today. Thankfully, I figured out a better way to capture someone's attention.

I'll share with you the story of how I managed to finally get it right. When we change our focus from our Why to our Who; it helps us achieve our dreams and goals. I've seen it happen in the business right after seeing it work in my most important relationship.

The One Strategy that Landed Me the One

In my early thirties, I was able to redeem my years of bad dating experiences. A friend introduced me to a girl named Hayley. I was told that she was both beautiful and intelligent - two powerful credentials I must admit. Right from the outset, I was determined to get a different outcome than the brokenness I had left in the past. I didn't want to screw up this time. I started by committing in meeting number one to shutting up and taking a genuine interest in Hayley's life.

As part of my new approach, I began collecting some information on her. Many would call this "due diligence." Some might call it creepy. Whatever you want to call it, it worked because it got me away from only thinking about myself.

On our first date, I learned about her budding career as a teacher. That was my in to start a string of questions about her passions in life. I realized she loved teaching children. She mentioned it was an excellent career for raising a family. We had plenty to talk about as the time flew by. The two of us aligned on the idea that strong families and fantastic teachers are pillars of a great society. We had so much more to talk about. As time went on that night, our conversation switched to discussing the next date. The plan was working.

For the next date, I started asking about her parents, siblings, extended family, friends, neighbors, and pretty much anybody she ever knew. Her answers sparked my curiosity and led to more questions. I wanted to learn as much about Hayley as I could. I took many mental notes. Later I would transfer these onto an ongoing note I kept on my phone.

By the time we went on our fourth date, my inquisitive boldness was at an all-time high.

I summoned the courage to ask one night, "Hayley, what's your favorite food?" She said, "Lasagna." Wanting to add layers to my ever-growing list of facts about her, I asked a prodding follow-up question:

"What do you like about lasagna?"

As it turns out, she appreciated the meat to cheese to noodle ratio the most.

Later she confessed my question went too far and nearly disqualified me into the "Creepy Guy" category. Point taken. I justified the question knowing I was compiling an impressive database of information. Sure, one *could* interpret this as weird. But if she found out at the right time, it could also be seen as a very romantic gesture. Relationships are risky like that.

One day I was reading through my list and realized that this was the girl for me. In the process, I also realized that if I spent my life making all Hayley's now well-documented dreams a reality, I could achieve my goals of leading a happy family as well. Not long after, I decided that I would devote my life helping her experience the life she always wanted.

Today, we are over ten years married with three beautiful girls. They keep us busy and laughing all the time. Often, at the end of a long but rewarding day, we remark to each other that while

Impacting a Who is more effective than trying to talk about my Why all the time.

it's never easy, we are living out our dream, one day at a time. As mentioned, this new approach to dating was a catalyst for the "Start With Who" business strategy I lay out in this book.

While we've been putting together a great love story, I can see that my new methodology of winning someone over was a brilliant sales strategy.

Start With Why...Then Start Again With Who

In *Start With Why*, Sinek effectively convinces his readers that every person, organization, or company needs a deep-seated purpose. The Why is their cause or belief that they are working to achieve. A Why could also be a problem in the world they aspire to solve.

For those who struggled to define a "Why," Sinek co-wrote a follow-up book titled, *Find Your Why: A Practical Guide For Discovering Purpose For You And Your Team*[2].

This accompanying book helped readers look to their passions, experiences, struggles, etc., to tease out some themes that could lead to a "Why" statement.

I clarified my Why. But there was still something missing.

Once the assigned exercise is complete, anyone should know why they're motivated as they are.

I excitedly read the book and did the prescribed exercises. I clarified my Why. But I still felt something was missing.

People nodded their heads politely when I told them about my Why. However, a polite agreement doesn't mean they would come along for the journey to help me achieve it. My pitches fell flat. I didn't sell books as I wanted. My talks didn't land like I thought they should have.

It didn't take long before realizing that "Start With Why" and "Find Your Why" needed a follow-up. I couldn't be the only one that felt this way.

I did a quick Google search to see if anyone else was writing in line with my discontent about the "Start With Why" phenomenon. I found that Ken Krogue, in a post for Forbes[3], made an argument that when it comes to achieving significant sales, finding the *right person* was more important than talking about your Why. Krogue was the first person (and one of the only ones) on the Internet that I saw asking the question,

"Why not start with Who instead?"

I'm not convinced that Krogue had it fully right, either. He argues that getting your Who right always precedes achieving your Why. The logical outworking of his argument is:

First, find people with whom you connect. Next, discover your purpose as you help them.

This is where I disagree with Krogue. I'm with Sinek on this one that our Why is foundational to the reason we show up and work up each day. Once we have our Why clear, *then* we find the people that we can help. Without a Why leading us, we are in danger of becoming what Zig Ziglar called a "wandering generality."[4] Wandering Generalities are the people who aspire to greatness by trying to reach everyone. They may get large followings but a cursory survey of their lack of impact reveal their work to be a mile wide and an inch deep.

Instead, Ziglar encouraged leaders to become a "meaningful specific." This is where you become something special to an intentional group of people. I prefer this approach. I have never wanted to be a celebrity, but I have always known that I wanted to maximizc my impact on the most amount of lives.

Is Liking People Just For Extroverts?

Helping people has always been the fuel that drives me as a professional. This book's message - that recovering a passion for serving and helping people, does not surprise my friends and family who saw me grow up. In school, I was terrible with math and science. I barely passed the bare minimum graduation requirements. It was the same experience while working through my MBA. I have always struggled with accounting and finance classes. On the other hand, I loved any learning that involved people. I loved studying the social sciences (psychology, sociology), playing team sports, and sharing ideas with friends.

Does that mean I'm an extrovert? Not at all. Even those closest to me mistake my love for people for extroversion. Believe me, it's not being an extrovert that fuels my love for people. It's even insulting to introverts to suggest that the way they recharge alone means they don't like people. My confidants are often surprised to learn that I too need significant amounts of time alone to feel like a healthy contributor to society. Rather, my passion for people comes from my beliefs about the nature of humanity. Additionally, I've seen in history and from my mentors that a career devoted to serving people is the path to a life of joy and significance.

Where I Learned About Loving People

For years, I cut my vocational teeth by serving in a local church. It is leading in a church where I sharpened my skills in how to create a culture of service. The church is one place where we need to learn how to love people better. As one given the mantle of "leader", I knew I needed to model it myself. But I couldn't personally care for everyone myself. When you're the pastor of a large church, there's a crisis of limitation built into the job description. You can't be there to care for everyone with the attention they all deserve. As a leader, however, you can work hard to create an organization and culture where everyone feels valued and cares for each other. When a church is full of people who care for others, it can be a dynamic presence in their community.

But love doesn't always come naturally for any organization. Creating an organization like this starts with developing strategies around the philosophical beliefs and values that *people are worth caring for*. Many of us know this intrinsically.

Like the church, the business world has a few things to learn about how critical people are to its existence (and growth). Today, I have transferred my focus to serving entrepreneurs and business leaders. I help them restore a passion for serving humanity through their work. When they do this, their lives, their business and their communities at large are rewarded.

If you're struggling to make the jump from "Why" to "Win", you may have a people problem. You will appreciate the challenge coming in the pages that follow. If you know you are destined for more impact than you are currently making, this book is for you.

In order to get across the Why to Win chasm, you need a bridge. Serving other people is how you are going to do just that. Together we will see that there are very intentional steps to take to get to where you want to go. You'll be inspired by some amazing business leaders who took those very steps en route to crossing the chasm and winning their story.

It's Tough To Achieve Your Why

After my time as a pastor, I began my second career as a marketing consultant. I took my passion for people and applied it to growing businesses.

I realized that many companies have great Why's, but that doesn't guarantee sales, profits, and growth - the things they need to scale their Why.

Let's go back to Brad, the struggling bachelor in Simon Sinek's example. Imagine Brad applied his dating strategy to his company's sales and marketing. It still wouldn't work. We all know why.

The problem is that leading with and sharing your "Why" does not capture attention in our noisy world.

In dating and business, human psychology is similar: *People don't care about you as much as you care about yourself.*

Of course, our moms care about our Why. Our spouses pretend to care about our Why. But the real people we need to reach in business, the ones who pay our bills and help us achieve our goals - they really don't care to hear about our Why.

I'm not alluding to mean people. Even the kindest, most benevolent saints out there aren't thinking about us like we think they should. They've got enough to think about already. They're consumed by trying to figure out their own *Whys*. They've got busy lives. Their lives full of problems that they're working hard to solve to make their stories work out for them.[5]

I understand how frustrating it can be to be passionate about your purpose and yet struggle to get others on board.

Impacting your Who is connected to achieving your Why.

If you profoundly impact the people I'm calling your "Who," then you can achieve your Why.

When it comes to your business, embracing the Why is a major component to success. But you'll never get your Why unless you are wholly devoted to serving a Who.

Both Why and Who matter but for different reasons.

Climb The Mountain, Discover Your Why, Come Home, And Then Start With Who

Some people think I'm kicking off this book by throwing shade on Simon Sinek. That's not the case at all. There's nothing wrong with healthy disagreement. Our culture needs to learn how to disagree respectfully. I think everyone should embrace the "Start With Why" framework for which Sinek is famous. We could all benefit from taking the time to figure out our Why. I highly encourage it.

You could schedule an epic quest to discover your Why. Climb a mountain to get inspired. Don't return until you figure out *why* you exist (your purpose, mission, values, etc. - all the things that Sinek recommends). Now you know your purpose. Now it's the time to direct your energy to achieve it.

Now it's time to come back down, get to work, and Start With Who.

When you return, don't assume people will want to hear about what you learned while you were gone. None of us were up there with you. We didn't share your mountaintop experience. We've been stuck in the valley, and trying to make it down here is the only thing on our minds.

Why People Don't Listen To Us

Your Why is personal.

Remember when you came back from that exciting trip and quickly became discouraged when the people you talked to seem bored and disinterested after a few minutes of telling your stories? Except for those closest to us, most people don't care, nor do they have time to hear about everything we've seen or done. Strangers, acquaintances, and Uber drivers may politely give us a couple of minutes of their time but not much more before they glaze over.

I recall the year I spent studying at the University of Oxford. If ever there was an interesting place, Oxford is it. I spent a year sitting under some of the best minds, engaging in life-changing conversations, and being a part of stories that I could share for hours. When I got home, much to my surprise, no one seemed as interested in my time there as I was. That year, I visited Auschwitz, walked around Stonehenge, participated in the search for a lost city in a Middle Eastern archeological dig, and won a prestigious award for my Varsity Match performance against the University of Cambridge in ice hockey.

Interesting stuff, right?

When I came home, I thought I'd have lineups of people waiting to talk about what they had seen me do on social media. They didn't. Family members had already heard the stories on the phone. Old friends wanted instead to spend the time laughing about the shared memories we had growing up. New friends wanted to create new memories. I couldn't get into it with strangers. Unless it's about drama in the royal family, most North Americans can't be bothered with what's going on in the UK (and I understand that).

I'd say most people I talk to regularly have no idea about my experiences in England. The truth is that their ambivalence doesn't bother me one bit. I know people have their own stories of adventure, struggle, and achievement. I don't have the time to listen to their' experiences either. Not having time to listen to each other is a symptom of a bigger problem outside the scope of this book.

Assuming that you're going to have ample opportunities to share your "Why" is setting yourself up for disappointment. Don't expect to come down from your quest hoping to show up to sold-out theatres full of people waiting to hear about why you're here.

The same principle applies to your business. I want to show you the trouble with trying to do marketing like people try to impress others - by just talking about yourself.

How to Sell a Tide Pen

What happens when you try to market your product, service, or idea and lead with your "Why"?

Let's look at the difference between *Starting With Why* vs. *Starting With Who* as it pertains to how you might pitch a product.

Imagine for a moment that you work in the marketing department for the detergent giant, Tide. Your team is trying to sell their new "detergent in a pen" product. In this imaginary scenario, you're knee-deep in a routine marketing meeting. Seeking a new marketing campaign for a new year, the top thinkers all chime in to offer a slant of the company's "Why." They get together with you and your team in a boardroom and start brainstorming ideas.

The chair of the meeting puts a question before the group,

 Okay, everyone, we have been leading this industry for years. We need a fresh message that will take this company into the future. What can we say to convince the masses to choose Tide over our competitors?

One person puts their hand up: "Remember how we were one of the first detergents on the market designed to fight stains. Let's tell people that *we are innovators*."

There is agreement around the room as heads nod.

Another adds, "Let's tell our story. We should film a commercial about how we've been perfecting our stain-fighting detergent for sixty years now. *We have proven expertise in stain removal*."

The executives all love it. There is a clear consensus while the room starts to bubble with excitement.

Another adds, "And as far as I know, no one here has ever been to jail. That means (motioning to write letters in the sky) '*We can be trusted.'"*

Thinking they are really onto something, another partner stands up and shouts, *"And we are the number one brand recommended by washing machine companies!"*

The room erupts in chanting and whisks the VP of Marketing out in a hero's parade to celebrate over drinks.

"We're number one! We're number one!" can be heard echoing through the office as they leave.

The scribe taking notes is left in the room alone, thinking that this message doesn't resonate with her. Regardless, she pens her summary and forwards it to the advertising department for next year's campaign with a grimace:

 Buy our pen because we are the number one, innovative, and trustworthy detergent company recommended by washing machine companies... and we are very proud of it.

Who is inspired by this campaign? It's a tired tactic that takes zero creativity and total narcissism. It's the same tactic used by the guy on the first date who only wants to talk about how amazing he is.

This example identifies one of the significant flaws of starting with "Why." People get put off by another company talking about themselves. The problem with this campaign is that it is all about them. There's nothing about what Tide does for the benefit of the consumer.

What if, hypothetically, *I* was their target market? Let's examine how starting with Who can produce different results.

One Of My Nightmares

Starting instead with Who considers first the intended audience. It captures *their* attention by highlighting a specific problem the audience is struggling to overcome.

If I'm the targeted customer of this company (their Who), here's a better way to capture my attention. I don't care about their awards or years of service. I care about keeping my shirts clean.

It's the morning of the big presentation. I have spent hours researching and going through every detail of my upcoming talk. I have read it out loud to myself in front of the mirror multiple times. While I get great reactions from the audience in the mirror, the talk remains unproven to real-life audiences.

I say "goodbye" to my wife and kids, pulling out of the driveway like a soldier going into battle. In a few minutes, I'll be going through the drive-thru of my coffee shop to get another dose of liquid inspiration. My favorite coffee is now riding shotgun with me. Together, we are off to conquer the world.

As I navigate the route and weave through traffic, I feel confident that I have selected the right sports coat (casual but still professional) with a matching shirt. I bring no spare shirt. Why would I? You can't have two favorite shirts. Besides, what could go wrong? I am listening to my go-to motivational playlist, take a sip, and tragedy hits. My mouth has failed to make the perfect connection with the lid opening.

I've spilled my coffee. It's not all the coffee. A few drips. But that's enough to stand out for sure.

In a moment, my confidence has vanquished. For the rest of the day, I'll be convinced that *everyone* is noticing and focusing on the coffee spots on my shirt.

My swagger is gone.

Giving the presentation stressed me out enough. Now I have stains that not even my jacket will cover. My anxiety level has just maxed out.

What would ease the stress?

There exists a pen that discharges laundry detergent instead of conventional ink!

This pinnacle of human innovation assures me that no matter what substance may hit my shirt, I could get it off with that magical, patented, translucent fluid.

I keep one of those pens in my car in an unconventional act of wisdom. I have lived through this nightmare and wish not to repeat it. I should keep two around because one in the laptop bag never hurts either.

The guys in that marketing meeting should've directed their campaign away from themselves. They could have targeted coffee-loving, favorite-shirt-wearing business people who desire to drink their morning coffee with boldness.

Who doesn't face the threat of a coffee stain every morning commute? Who couldn't benefit from the ease of knowing that any stain is no match for the power of a disaster-erasing pen?

By turning their eyes and focusing on this kind of situation, they would get our attention. If you work for Tide and are reading this, you can have that one for free.

That's the power of a compelling narrative rather than just talking about yourself.

In summary, what's the difference between the above two approaches when selling a stain-removing pen? There's a complete difference in perspective with the hero of the stories: It's about *Why vs. Who*. The first story focused on the company's Why. They were the focus, and nobody cared. The second looked at the transformation the product could offer a customer by casting *the consumer* as their message's focus.

That, to me, is a much more effective approach.

Starting With Who Is About Identifying Problems And Then Showing How You Can Help Solve Them

What if, in your journey to spread *your* ideas, you got up each day and instead of shouting, "Look at me! Listen to my story! See how great I am!" you thought:

"Who am I helping win today?"

This kind of message works. It's how you create raving fans of your brand.

It is the most effective way to present your ideas, so they impact the marketplace, and you make the income you are looking for - you start with Who.

Maybe you have an idea that you want other people to buy into, grow a business, or advance a cause close to your heart.

"Who am I helping win their story today?"

If this is the case, you already know what your Why is. The challenge then becomes achieving it. Could it be possible to achieve your Why, you will have to be open to the idea of discovering and focusing on your Who? To do this, we need to take our eyes off ourselves, maybe even swallow some pride and keep our mouths shut. In some cases, this won't be easy. Serving your Who is the only way to make your Why a reality.

How To Get Others To Buy-In To Your Ideas

Here's what we know about busy consumers today: They only listen when there is something of benefit to them. If they listen, they are only being cordial and waiting for the part where they get some advantage.

If you read *Start With Why*, you would think that every business transaction is an exchange of core values. Simon Sinek argues that we should only give our money to companies with whom we agree on fundamental core values.

When is the last time you said to yourself before making a purchase, "Before I buy this, I want to make sure I agree with this company's core values"?

Granted, a boycott may happen from time to time when a company achieves notoriety, making the news because of a newsworthy indiscretion. We have every right to boycott. But here I'm talking about the bulk of your consumer decisions. Do you know the Why of the company that made your vacuum cleaner, breakfast cereal, or the car you drive?

Not likely.

You bought those things for what they do for you. They looked good, were on sale, or made you feel good.

Why People Buy Stuff

People buy products and services because it solves a problem for them. In most cases, it's not because the manufacturer or supplier has a resonating core value.

Simon Sinek reiterates this familiar chorus throughout Start With Why,

 People don't buy what you do; they buy why you do it.

I don't think that's true.

Sinek's suggestion that people only buy your Why is overstepping. It's giving people too much credit for what motivates their decisions. It's assuming we're all taking the time to do something that we all know we don't have time to do.

Here's my confession: I don't have a clue what the core values are for the vast majority of the vendors I purchase products and services from either personally or to run my business.

The last time I bought a power tool, my first thought was not to go to Home Depot's website and read their "About" page to see what the company's mission statement was.

I just needed a drill. That's it. I didn't need a cultural manifesto.

There is one thing that motivates consumers. It comes from business guru, Michael Hyatt. Hyatt teaches that we consumers are tuned into the radio station *W.I.I.FM* (That is, *"What's in It for Me?"*). We make purchases for four reasons:

1. We think something solves a problem for us.
2. It makes our life easier.
3. It helps us to become better people.
4. It satisfies an inner desire to be identified in a particular way.

It's Not Your Why; It's Me

I make purchases of products and services because they promise to help me overcome something I am facing.

A company's *Why* almost never crosses my mind. Neither when I am logging on to an e-commerce site or walking around a brick-and-mortar store. I buy things not because I'm a benevolent consumer trying to save the world and help a CEO achieve their Why. I make purchases because what they're offering helps me get what I need to win that day.

As a consumer, the big question that I need to have answered is: *did the brand connect with me so that I knew they would solve a problem I was facing?*

Do you think people buy Apple products because they love Apple's Why and want to help them become the most prominent company globally? For the hardcore Apple people, that could be true. These are the people who line up for a week before any new product is released. But for the vast majority of iPhone users, my guess is "That's not me." Most iPhone users haven't even read the "Terms and Conditions" they've signed, never mind Apple's mission or vision statement.

Do you know the mission, vision, or values of what drives Apple Inc.? If you don't, that's ok. Most people don't. Most of us buy Apple products because of what these products do for us.

Apple is best known for offering user-friendly technology that enables millennials, soccer moms, kids, and grandparents to leverage technology's power.

Apple has done a brilliant job of building a community that enjoys sparking conversations about their purchases and experiences. If you have a couple of free hours, go to any coffee shop at any hour of the day and start looking around. Ask all the people with the glowing Apples on their laptops a question about their beloved Apple product. They'll shut down whatever they were doing and tell you all about it. This is the validation they have been craving all day! They love to expound on how excellent their own tech choices are.

Note that it's not the Why they rave about Apple. It's all about what Apple does for them. That's why they bought the product. And then, next launch next year, they'll come running back for that same rush again.

Apple may be Sinek's poster child for doing "Why" well. I argue that without appealing to their Who, Apple would have never accumulated its cult-like millions of happy customers.

Regardless of their Why, I personally am looking forward to the new iPhone - whenever it comes, whatever it looks like — I'll be ready.

Now Shift from Why to Who

Suppose you want to get from "Why" to "Win" you absolutely must Start With Who to get you there. Ideas spread, connections get made, and influence grows when we get over ourselves and focus on serving the people we're trying to reach.

In Dale Carnegie's classic book, *How to Win Friends and Influence People*[6], one of the primary principles Carnegie shares is that to win people over, you must see things from another's point of view. In other words, knowing your Who is imperative because if you don't know or understand your Who, you will advertise, market, and communicate from your Why and perspective.

The late Carnegie further expounds the value of Who by encouraging the reader to appeal to the other person's inner desires and wants. By adopting this approach, convincing someone

When nobody seems to care about your Why, try starting with Who.

your product or service is in their best interest becomes much more manageable.

If you're frustrated because nobody seems to care about your Why, it's now time to rethink your approach to people. We could all learn a lesson in loving people again. That's the next step towards winning your Why.

---

1. Sinek, Simon. *Start With Why* (Penguin Books, 2009). p 77
2. Sinek, Simon, Docker, Peter, & Mead, David. *Find Your Why: A Practical Guide For Discovering Purpose For You And Your Team* (Harlow, Eng). Penguin Books, 2017.
3. See Simon Sinek Says 'Start With Why,' But Sales Experts Disagree" Ken Krogue. Full article: https://www.forbes.com/sites/kenkrogue/2015/07/06/simon-sinek-says-start-with-why-but-sales-experts-disagree/#6631274b4b82
4. *See* https://www.ziglar.com/quotes/meaningful-specific. Accessed April 5, 2021.
5. For a powerful treatment of this idea, I recommend the book, Building A StoryBrand by Don Miller. (HarperCollins Leadership, 2017).
6. Carnegie, Dale, *How To Win Friends and Influence People*. New York:Simon & Schuster, 2009.

THREE

Love People And Help Them Win

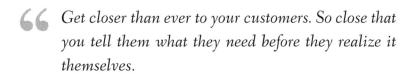

Get closer than ever to your customers. So close that you tell them what they need before they realize it themselves.

- Steve Jobs

How far would you go to help one of your customers? This example of customer service sets the bar high.

I didn't have to go further than my favorite hot dog vendor in town to meet the hero of this story.

It's a heart-warming story of how far a hot dog vendor would go to love a customer. Andrew "Skully" White is the owner of Lully's Food Experience. It's a gourmet hot dog stand in a Canadian Tire parking lot in Abbotsford, B.C. It's also happens to be my favorite hot dog joint in town.

For three years, Tim Hiscock was a regular customer of Lully's. Hiscock and White never knew each other's first names, but they still bonded over the love of good food and sports.

That relationship nearly came to a screeching halt when Tim Hiscock's kidneys were nearing complete failure, a complication of living with Type 1 diabetes. Hiscock had recently taken a turn for the worse. The doctors prescribed a strict diet and drastic measures to be taken for him to survive. Hiscock's wife went to Scully, explained his kidney condition, and pleaded with the hotdog vendor to stop selling her husband his weekly hotdog.

"We told him that we just found out that Tim needed a new kidney," Hiscock's wife told a reporter in an interview. "Skully asked what was involved in donating a kidney. We told him the donor had to have a matching blood type. He [Skully] quickly threw in, 'If I'm a match, you can have mine.'"

"I knew you could live off of one, and I asked him, what's the criteria?" Skully commented when asked.

It turned out the pair was a blood match, and Skully committed to the transplant within days.

"It's a cool journey. For me to be able to yank something out of me while I'm alive and stick it into him? And it works. It's the coolest," he said.

"If you've got two healthy kidneys, give one up and save somebody," White said. It was the most amazing feeling in the world that I could do this for him."[1]

In another article, Skully White was asked by a reporter why he'd donate a kidney to a customer whose name he didn't even know. His response was indicative of someone who had a love for humanity:

"Why not?"[2]

I get the sense that if Skully had six kidneys, he would have given them all.

For The Love Of Customers (And Humanity)

I'm not asking that we take Skully's lead and offer a kidney to all our top customers. I'm merely asking that you care about the essential people that keep your business alive, your customers.

It saddens me that the public have come to expect poor customer service from most establishments.

This is because many businesses have lost their love for humanity. This lack of love is reflected in poor care of their customers. We've all experienced the disappointment of a business that didn't go the extra mile for us. How do you avoid doing it to your customers?

Many businesses start with compassion for customers and their plight. Startups and small companies can go above and beyond to offer rockstar service. Under relentless pressure to keep the machine profitable, little compromises happen along the way. These include:

- produce quick profits at the expense of quality
- automate systems at the expense of personal service
- hit goals to earn promotions
- cut corners to improve PNL in order to appease shareholders

Customer care suffers when businesses work so hard to hit short term goals and we compromise product quality, embrace sleazy sales tactics, trim services, and stack on more unexpected fees to customers to squeeze a few more dollars out of them. In exchange for the quick win, the customer pays for it. This may work for the present annual report. Over time, however, the company that relentlessly reduces value and squeezes more money out of their customers will pay for it later.

The commitment to add profit by adding value is a core conviction that you can't create by simply writing it on the office wall or posting it on your website. It comes from your driving beliefs about why we serve other human beings.

If you don't get this right, your brand will suffer if it's not already. The modern consumer comes with a built-in Tupperware detector - they can smell plastic from a mile away. Because of this, every company needs the right mindset and care for other human beings to succeed.

How do you feel about this question: *Are human beings a valuable gift to this world, or are they a resource to be exploited?*

You can't pretend to care. You have to really care. Sure, anyone can fake it for a while. But no one can fake it long enough to grow a business that makes enduring income and impact.

If we are honest, too many of us don't care about people like we know we should. We can give all kinds of lip service about the importance and power of love, tolerance, and acceptance. If we're honest, people annoy us too easily. Does it seem like we've done everything to protect ourselves from this "annoyance" by eliminating human interaction from day-to-day life?

We have self-checkout to avoid cashiers.

We have ATMs to avoid bank tellers.

The delivery guys used to knock on the door and chat for a few minutes. Now they drop off the package and take off immediately.

As with society, so with our businesses. We automate and delegate ourselves out of the customer experience.

While productivity hacks are wonderful gifts to efficiencies, they can become the beginning of our business losing touch with the heartbeat of business - the people we help.

Business is a microcosm of the rest of our lives. Remember how miserable we got when we were isolated in lockdown?

When COVID lockdowns started happening, many thought it was novel - a little people-break for the introverted.

"A couple of weeks at home doesn't sound so bad," we thought.

By the winter of 2020, six months into the pandemic, we were devastated with the second wave surging. First, social gatherings caused us to stay home (this time, it was much less welcomed). Then it was Thanksgiving that got "canceled." Then Christmas. By this point, no one thought being cut off from their friends and family was fun or novel anymore. We missed the packed football games, the ugly-sweater parties, and just being with people. We missed hugging our loved ones.

We felt distant. We felt alone.

It's no surprise that mental health deteriorated to a crisis level in many communities during this season.

The COVID lockdowns reminded us of how important people were to our personal health - even the introverts figured it out.

The years of 2020 and 2021 were a wake up call that connecting with people is essential to living a healthy life. The car, house, and holidays may make life fun, but they do not make for a rewarding life. Nobody ever goes to their deathbed wishing to get one more hug in from their vehicle or their stock portfolio.

If you can get this right, you will have both joy and success in life and businesses. People are tough to have around, for sure. But we've all learned that we'd rather the problems that come from having them around than the problems that come with not having them.

Let's examine the state of your heart in regards to how you feel about people, more specifically, your customers.

It's About Truly Caring For People

If you get this part right, you'll have a new outlook on people. The bridge to winning in business and achieving your Why depends on genuinely caring for people.

It has to be something that everyone values - they cannot just put it on a website, placard, or billboard. You have to really mean it. Let's talk about the condition of your heart towards other human beings.

"People Are More Important Than Things"

My late grandpa, or "Papa," as we called him, was and still is a hero of mine. Though he died when I was only twelve, he was around for much of my early childhood. He was an engaged grandpa. He was there to offer unsolicited grandfatherly wisdom to any impressionables who would listen. I remember the car rides I took with him on the way to hockey games, church, or while running various errands together. He proudly drove his old Buick with a cigar in his mouth. Papa was a talker. I call these moments "skyscraper drives" - it was story upon story upon story upon story.

I confess now that his insight then fell on deaf ears at the time. His word has become appreciated in my life through my twenties, thirties, and now into my forties.

In a recent visit with my mom, she pulled out a tribute that I had written for Papa as an early teenager. I wrote this two years after he lost his battle with lung cancer. It's incredible to me the trivial things moms hold onto can become uncovered and even make it into a book decades later.

As I read the tribute, I was taken back in time. The document resurrected memories that I thought were lost. My writing celebrated Papa's love for people. I knew even then how special it was that I got to have that time with him.

People are more important than things.

Here's what he taught me the most. It's the heartbeat of this business book:

Jono," as he called me, "people are more important than things."

Papa would often recite this phrase when we were together. I used to roll my eyes; we heard it so often. I'd give anything to hear him repeat it in person.

Nostalgia aside, Papa was right. People *are* more important than things.

By his standard, the measure of a successful life was found not to accumulate material items. Rather, Papa taught me how we determine a life of significance by the positive and transformative impact we made on other people. Though he died much too early, I see how my grandpa passed his values on to me. His words of wisdom serve as a guiding star that leads me through challenges and temptations of life. They are at the core of how I run my businesses. His message has ultimately become the primary message of this book:

 The heart of your business has to be about people because people are more important than anything else.

Business Is About Loving People

One of the things I love about business is that you have to love people to be good at it.

Did you have to read that again? It's true. Your business exists because you have a mandate to love people and help them. As entrepreneurs and business leaders, we don't have to shout it on the news or write it on some cardboard at a rally. We do have to show it each day we arrive at work.

And when you do that in business, you are rewarded for it.

It's the responsibility of people, not the government, to help each other out. Too many of us observe problems in the news or read something troubling in our social media feeds. We look around at our broken communities and hope someone else does something to solve these issues.

Many look to a government program to rid the world of wrong. They blame past or current political leadership for society's ills, hoping that "their person" will make it better next time.

That's not how it works. The government has neither the resources, creativity, speed, track record, or the soul to bear the mantle of "universal problem solver."

It's our responsibility as humans to solve problems for each other.

We have to care for each other. I'm convinced that business is part of the divine plan for making his world better. When we do an excellent job of helping people, we are rewarded with the gift of money.

We Need People In Any And Every Business

To run a profitable business, we need people around us to varying degrees. Regardless of how talented or brilliant, or hard-working we are, we need people around to make it a success. Without the right people, our business or idea will not catch on.

If you're going to have people around, you might as well learn to care about them. You might even enjoy them for the value they can bring to your life in return.

You may think people annoy you. I get that. But I bet that you are more of a people person than you think. Here are some questions to tell that you aren't as ornery about other people as you think you are:

- After awhile, did you miss being around people during the COVID lockdown?
- During lockdown, did you find yourself watching old clips of large events and miss the days you could be around crowds of people?
- Do you get a buzz from going to conferences where "your kind of people" gather? Even just a little buzz?
- Do you drive or fly through snowstorms during the holidays to reconnect with your spreadsheets or loved ones?
- Have you ever grieved when you watched the news and grieved a great loss of human life?
- Do your best-kept memories involve the nights you spent binge-watching TV alone or the ones you spent with people?
- If a hurricane or fire was approaching your house, would you run inside to grab photos of your car or of people?

It's always about people.

Try this: When you think about your years at work, what are the highlights that come to mind?

It's all about the people. Customers and coworkers are what we remember most.

People are the jewel of life. When we are far from connecting with other people, loneliness creeps into our hearts and makes life incredibly miserable.

My Struggle With Loneliness

Loneliness carries a particular sting that cuts us deep.

I experienced a memorable moment like this on a trip that took me halfway around the world. At a time that I should have felt immeasurable happiness, I felt incredible loneliness.

Traveling alone many years ago, I stopped in Paris on a layover en route to Africa. I was joining a group doing some intense work building an orphanage and wanted to get in some sight-seeing before the big push. Since I was traveling alone to Africa, I reviewed my travel itinerary and was pleasantly surprised. Once I landed in London, I saw a layover that would allow me to cross an item off my bucket list:

Get a picture standing in front of the Eiffel Tower.

When I landed, I quickly found a locker to stash my luggage

and then made a beeline to a train that would take me across the English Channel and into Paris.

Once in Paris, I grabbed a cab to Champ De Mars. I scouted out a picturesque place to capture a moment with the world-renowned landmark. I was excited. I felt a rush of satisfaction upon arrival, knowing I would forever have this picture.

Bucket list item: *Check!*

Taking out my trusty 35mm (that's what we used to call a camera when they didn't come with a phone attached), I placed it on the ground facing the iconic tower. I set the timer and positioned myself, striking my best pose.

I got the picture. I fulfilled the mission. There was a moment of euphoria.

And then... the feeling was gone.

Suddenly I felt something I never felt this strong before. While I had achieved a life milestone, I had no one to share the moment with. There was no one around to high five.

I was all alone.

I was on a tight schedule and needed to get back to the airport. I hailed a cab and headed back across the channel to the airport. Of course, my driver didn't speak any English. He seemed to be tuned into classic rock (in English). The song that came on during the drive was *Desperado* by the Eagles.

Desperado is the loneliest song ever written.

"Mauvais Quart D'heure."

Later I realized I lived out the French expression, which translated means "bad quarter of an hour."

I won't forget the sting of loneliness that hit me that day. I was at one of the most beautiful, and most romantic places in the world. And it was soured by having the experience alone.

Reflecting on this moment, I realized that no matter how incredible the experience is, it loses its impact if other people aren't involved. It's like that in travel, at home, and in business.

It's people that make a life meaningful.

It's the people, not towers or exotic travel, that make life the most meaningful.

Here's an illustration with which we can relate. Open up the photo app on your phone and scroll through the moments you've captured. As you're scrolling, take note of the ones that make you pause and take a second look. Which images cause you to linger? I can guess already. It's the ones with the people in it. Architecture, mountains, oceans, rivers, and trees all have their beauty, but nothing grips our attention like human beings.

Further to the point, have a look at the photos you've posted on social media that receive the most engagement. It's the ones with faces, not the landmarks or geography.

The lesson: *People naturally connect with other people.*

Putting People First

I saw the power of what putting people first can do for you during my days as a pastor. Even as a young man, I had the privilege of spending time with people in their final moments on Earth. I was there for those mysterious, sacred moments where they breathe their last breath and pass from this life to the next. In all my times doing this, I never visited someone's deathbed and heard them request to be surrounded by piles of their money or material things. The things we spend so much of our lives pursuing do not console us when we're facing the end of our lives.

We will talk more about that in the next chapter.

Business Is About Helping People Win

You will soon discover that every great business has put other people at the center. Humans are unavoidable.

As Don Miller points out in *Building A StoryBrand*, every business is H2H – human to human.[3] We are all people trying to help other people win. Your platform may be marketed or sold as Business to Business (B2B) or Business to Consumer (B2C). Still, at the core, you are a human doing business with other humans. There's always a human behind every buying or selling transaction.

What If There Were No People?

I know that you've probably thought it before. Maybe you've even yelled it out in a moment of frustration:

"I'd like this job a lot more if there weren't any people in it!"

Peaceful as it may sound for a while, I know you wouldn't like it.

What kind of a world would it be if there weren't any people?

Imagine how hard Adam would have had it. Adam is the biblical character whom the Jews, Christians, and Muslims refer to as the first human. Based on your beliefs, you can call him whatever you'd like. Somebody had to come first and get a lay of the land so to speak. And this somebody had to deal with the fact that there was no one else around to help. When it was just one person, there were no other people around to help him solve problems. While this may seem like the introvert's dream, it took forever to do anything.

Here's why it was pronounced early on that it was "not good for man to be alone".[4]

Every time Adam wanted bread, it came at a high cost. First, he had to come up with the idea of farming. That would've been a significant milestone for even one person's lifetime of research. Then Adam had to take the time to grow his grain, water it, harvest it, thresh it, gather other ingredients, bake them all over a fire, and then cut his bread into uniform slices (we do know that "sliced bread" was a game-changing discovery to come many generations later).

Here's the point of my illustration: *Without other people running their businesses, Adam would have had to do everything himself.*

Thankfully, that's not the case today. There are people all over the world operating businesses that make our lives easier.

These people are showing up to work and serving people like you and I. We never see them. We never get to thank them personally. But they do it anyway. And you'd do it for them too. You probably do help them in one way or another in your business.

That's the power of people working together to serve each other.

What to Do When People Frustrate You

People can be frustrating. When people bother us, the temptation is to give up on the whole human race entirely. We enthusiastically declare:

"Forget all this talk about Who. I'm taking that first flight to Mars with Elon Musk and Richard Branson!"

I understand how the part of life that is most important also has the opportunity to do the most damage to us—the need for having a Who is something that none of us can escape.

People can hurt us deeply. But a life without any people would be a cold, depressing shell of an existence.

The great 20th-century author and Oxford scholar C.S. Lewis described the risk of relationships in his classic book *The Four Loves*:

 To love at all is to be vulnerable. Love anything, and your heart will be wrung and possibly broken. If you want to make sure of keeping it intact you must give it to no one, not even an animal. Wrap it carefully round with hobbies and little luxuries; avoid all entanglements. Lock it up safe in the casket or coffin of your selfishness. But in that casket, safe, dark, motionless, airless, it will change. It will not be broken; it will become unbreakable, impenetrable, irredeemable. To love is to be vulnerable.[5]

Lewis encourages us that no matter how much we've been hurt, burned by a bad deal, or betrayed by a partner, we cannot give up on having people in our lives. The cost of abandoning people is a cold, shrivelled heart. That, to me, is far worse than a broken one.

What If You Just Don't Care?

Imagine if you found out that your favorite Starbucks barista, the one fuelled on artificial enthusiasm from their endless supply of free coffee, didn't care about you? What if you found out that they only smiled when you came in and remembered your name and your personalized drink just because it was their job? What if you discovered after years of your generous tipping that they were pretending to be friendly with you. What if you discovered it was all an act to impress their manager and get promoted?

You'd be devastated.

What if your favorite company started screening your calls every time you showed up on their call display? Would you stay loyal to them? What if Amazon blocked your account or didn't accept returns because they came from you?

What would you do?

You'd stop giving them your business and find another company that did care. If that's how you feel about a company that doesn't care about you, why wouldn't one of your customers react the same if they found out you've lost your passion for serving.

In life and business, you are rewarded when you put people first.

Zig Ziglar famously said,

 You get all you want in life if you help enough other people get what they want.[6]

This proverb that has been providing business leaders wisdom for thousands of years:

A generous person will prosper; whoever refreshes others will be refreshed.[7]

In the above two quotes, Ziglar, the greatest sales coach, echoes the wise Solomon, one of the wealthiest men who ever lived, to teach us about the importance of putting others first as a foundation for success.

If you want to achieve your financial and lifestyle goals, the best way to do it is by helping people achieve theirs.

Another way I've been reiterating the same idea is "You get your Why, when you start with Who."

Let's Recapture Your Passion For People

Now Start With Who is about restoring awareness of how essential people are at every level of business.

Seth Godin writes of the significance of helping people in business:

 If you can bring someone belonging, connection, peace of mind, status, or one of the other most desired emotions, you've done something worthwhile. The thing you sell is simply a road to achieve those emotions, and we let everyone down when we focus on the tactics, not the outcomes. Who's it for and what's it for are the two questions that guide all of our decisions.[8]

The mindset Godin and I are calling for you to adopt does not come easily. You already know that anything worthwhile takes courage and hard work.

Personal relationships outside of business are challenging - that's why so many relationships become stagnant or die. I'm deeply committed to some of the most challenging relationships in the human experience. I'm married. I'm a father. I'm a son. I'm a son-in-law. I participate in discussions on social media. Telemarketers have my phone number.

All challenging relationships.

I also have clients whom I am committed to serving. Meaningful relationships require work. There are always going to be times of trials and obstacles to overcome.

Despite the difficulties that arise, the above are the most rewarding relationships in my life (except the telemarketers). To give up on them because they're difficult, tiring, frustrating, inconvenient, or a mix of any of those would be disastrous to the joy they bring.

Periodically, I may have a client with unreasonable demands and unrealistic expectations. I do what I can to make their experience a positive one. For every challenging client, the temporary frustration is overridden by the call, email, or even handwritten letter that says something along the lines of:

 We just wanted to drop you a quick line to let you know how much of a difference you have made in our business. The work you have done has increased our sales, increased engagement, and increased retention. We are so thankful we chose you and your team. Keep up the good work!

That email came from a client I almost gave up on. They challenged my love tolerance. Things got awkward at times. But we pressed through the difficulty and emerged stronger through it. Every relationship has conflict. That doesn't give us a pass to give up on them or the importance of relationships in general.

See New Leads With Eyes Of Compassion

As business owners, we know our customer's struggles. That's the market opportunity that got us into business in the first place. After working with them for a while, we start to see that we are the best solution for specific situations with which they're struggling. The problem is that they may not know we are best for them yet.

Before they meet you, they may hear all kinds of voices that sound like you during the sales cycle. These voices promise something similar, and sometimes for a better price. You may know your competitors are inferior, but this potential customer does not.

We wish they could just come to us first. Wouldn't it be so much easier if prospects came to us as innocent and optimistic as high school sweethearts? But they don't come to us like that. They often come as divorcees, a little hurt and a little jaded from previous bad experiences.

It's your job not to be angry at them for not seeing you as the obvious choice. We must compassionately show customers how your company, product, service, course, or whatever you provide will be the solution they need.

A Routine To Grow Empathy For People

I learned from a business mentor how to grow in empathy and tune in to a stranger's needs before ever meeting them. Before our first interaction, I spend a few minutes thinking about who they are and what they are currently going through. They reached out to us because something in their life is broken. They are hopeful that my company can help guide them out of the brokenness to a better situation.

Yes, it may be just about a website for which they could use some help. Maybe it is a marketing limitation they keep banging up against. To the business owner, it's just another Thursday morning. To them, however, it's a problem that's not going away on its own. Take a marketing agency, for example. What's really going on when someone reaches out to them because they have a marketing problem?

- Their leads are drying up
- They're watching competitors succeed
- They wonder if they can make payroll
- They're losing sleep at night due to an uncertain future
- It's holding them back from their goals and dreams

- It may even be affecting their other relationships at work and home

The marketing is never the only problem.

There's always a much bigger problem behind the problem. That's why we can have empathy when we're just meeting someone for the first time, and they could use some help.

Here's what helps me care for a stranger. I get in their proverbial shoes a bit and walk around in their life. I do some research on this person with whom I'm about to connect. I want to learn what I can about the origins of their business. I want to know their product and how they are currently communicating its value to the world. I check out their social media presence. I don't do this to be creepy. I do this because I'm curious about the person.

I want to learn as much as I can about who this unique being is with whom I'm about to cross paths.

I have found little nuances about individuals by seeing something they are interested in. Sometimes you can find a place they have visited or even a business periodical they read and recommended.

Some might think I am just trying to establish rapport and use sales psychology to win them over. It goes deeper than that. If I see something that gives me a chance to show empathy, it will help me connect with their humanity. When I know more about them, my heart warms up to the opportunity to do good in their life. And even if nothing is ever mentioned, subconsciously, I want them to know that I care about their situation. By this point, they are more than just a sales metric.

We Cannot Fake It Forever

Anyone can fake caring for customers for a few years. During that time, only a few will notice.

That customer has a story of being loved by friends, family, and God.

The problem is that if nothing changes, in a few years, *everyone will notice*.

If your heart was a gas gauge, would it be on "Full" or "Empty" regarding how much love you're feeling for others? If it's empty, you're going to struggle to care for customers as they deserve.

Take a moment to evaluate where your heart is at with people.

What do you need to do today to grow in love, compassion, and empathy? Perhaps you're still hanging on to something for which you need to let go.

This could be:

- A painful experience with someone you never fully dealt with
- A tough customer in the past that you haven't forgiven
- Or you're running too fast and not taking the time to care for people
- You're so motivated by sales and profits that you've forgotten that each customer is a life of value and dignity who needs help

We carry around unnecessary baggage from our past and bring it into every relationship in the present and future. It's time to let that stuff go. Whatever happened, recapturing that passion you once had to help people is something you'll need to lead a healthy life and business.

Conclusion

If you've lost that loving feeling with people, you might need to put the book down and do a heart check.

Your customer is a human being with friends, parents, children, brothers, and sisters. They are created and loved by God himself.

Do whatever you have to do to let a little compassion seep into your heart today. It will make you a better business person. Pray, meditate, or think about the preciousness of humanity so that when it's time to interact with the people, you elevate to a place where you do care about them.

Professional, you're there to help them in their time of need. They're more than another dollar sign to capture into your account. They are your Who. They have a story, a struggle, and they're looking for the very help you provide.

For them, it's chaos going on in their lives. For you, it's just another opportunity to show up and humbly serve.

The human heart was wired for relationships. People may bring issues but having no people around brings significantly more issues. In this chapter, we focussed on how even in business, we need to love people and help them win.

Helping a Who is always the first step on the way you go from Why to Win.

---

1. "Hot dog hero to donate kidney to customer". Glenda Luymes. Vancouver Sun., Vancouver, BC. November 6, 2020 https://vancouversun.-com/news/hotdog-hero-to-donate-kidney-to-customer
2. *Abbotsford kidney donor offers free hotdogs for life to other donors: Skully White, owner of Lullys Food Experience, donated his kidney to customer Tim Hiscock on Monday.* Scott Brown. *Vancouver Sun.* December 21, 2020. See article: https://vancouversun.com/news/abbotsford-kidney-donor-offers-free-hotdogs-for-life-to-other-donors
3. Miller, D. *Building a storybrand: Clarify your message so customers will listen.* New York: Harper Collins Leadership, an imprint of Harper-Collins, 2017.
4. See Genesis 2:18
5. Lewis, C.S. *The Four Loves.*Grand Rapids, Mich, HarperCollins, 1960 pp. 169
6. Ziglar, Z. *See you at the top.* Gretna: Pelican Pub, 1974.
7. Proverbs 11:25
8. Seth Godin, *This Is Marketing: You Can't Be Seen Until You Learn to See.* New York, NY: Penguin Books, 2018.

FOUR

Serving Is The New Selling

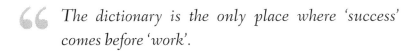

>> *The dictionary is the only place where 'success' comes before 'work'.*

- Unknown

Marian Wright Edleman was the first female African American to be admitted to the Mississippi Bar. With years of service, advocating for the overlooked in society, she leveraged her gifts. She worked tirelessly to support disadvantaged youth throughout the United States. Her impressive career included being the founder of the *Children's Defense Fund*. This fund offers children every opportunity to thrive through education, family welfare, justice, and other initiatives. What has driven Edleman to succeed?

She explains her mindset in her book, *The Measure of Our Success: A Letter to My Children and Yours,*

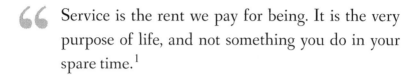 Service is the rent we pay for being. It is the very purpose of life, and not something you do in your spare time.[1]

Her now-famous line makes it clear that service to others is not optional. Service is a part of human existence, essential to our happiness and the happiness of others.

This is important if you want to break the drudgery of the work cycle. Have you ever wondered what your purpose was while you're at work? When you show up to work (wherever you work these days), you are never *just* an accountant, middle-manager, or freelancer. You are a servant to the good of others with whom you share the fellowship of humanity. The work you produce is part of a more incredible story. It's a story we are all telling as we serve each other with our work. You have a service. I have a service. Together we offer our services to the betterment of the world we share.

In the previous chapter, we looked at how we need to have the right philosophy of people to help us truly care for customers as they deserve. Now we shift to adopting a mindset of service. I believe that if we can get this point right, we can transform how business is depicted in society, especially the media.

Why People Are Skeptical About Business

Skepticism abounds regarding the evils of the corporate world. In most movies, the business guy representing "Corporate America" is usually more villain than a hero. When the public witnesses that narrative played out in film repeatedly, it shapes our friends, family and neighbours thinking that business and all who care about business are greedy and selfish. There are plenty of example of that, for sure. But it's certainly not true for everyone involved. Consider all the untold stories in your own business. Recall the customers you have helped over the years that never made the news - they never even made it to a Google review! You went above and beyond to make someone's day and no one else heard about it. You're not the only one to whom this happens. Every day, all over the world, people in need are getting outstanding help from people just like you in the business community. Whether they're in B2B or B2C, it's always humans serving other humans on some level.

There's a great deal of good being done. But because it doesn't fit the story that business is bad, we never hear about it.

I would argue that evil is not at the core of what business is all about. I believe there's a better story than the business world is telling every day.

The news media is doing no favors to the public perception of the business community. It too loves to report corporate corruption to shape cultural views. I challenge you to keep track for the next month of what kind of stories you witness reported in the news. Make a tally for each time business is portrayed as a positive force in society and how many times it is depicted as unfavorable. Remember that editors get to choose which stories to tell and which ones go untold. I believe there is a clear bias towards telling stories that are negative toward business.

The result is that we lose pride in our work. We get squeamish about talking about why we want to grow our business. We may even hold back sharing some good news that we know could serve the interest of many people for fear of being labeled one of the "bad sales guys who only wants to take other people's hard-earned money".

What if sales weren't such a bad thing? What if what we call "sales" was the act of offering something that someone badly needs? This is a fresh take on sales. The public may be skeptical about business. The public doesn't care for sales.

But we the public love being served.

That, to me, is the way back to winning public favor about what business is *actually* about.

In this chapter, I advocate for the idea that *serving is the new selling*. "Service" is a word that can is misunderstood, so we best define it properly.

You get your Why when you realize that service is one of the secret weapons of dynamic leaders. Winners are servers.

Service Is The New Sales

Do you remember what it was like to buy your first car? I vividly remember all the details of this monumental life stage.

Before we had the internet to browse from our pajamas, we had the newspaper. Dealerships posted tiny images of their used cars. To get a better idea of what they were offering, you had to show up to see it. I went over to a dealership a Saturday morning and started looking at cars in my price range.

As I was peering through the glass of one vehicle I liked, a cheery gentleman sauntered over to me and said, "That car has your name written all over it."

"Thank you," I replied...but I was certain he had no clue what my name was.

"Sam" (his name tag told me) followed me around the whole time. For the next thirty minutes, I felt like every move I made was being tracked and analyzed.

It got to be a little much. Eventually, I realized that Sam didn't care about which car was right for me. Sam would've been happy to see me drive away in any vehicle from the lot that day as long as his name was on the sheet as well. I could tell Sam didn't care what I cared about. Sam cared about his commission.

Since that day, I have always been uncomfortable around commission salespeople.

I meet lots of people who say that they don't like selling. Somebody like Sam gave them a bad experience. The word "selling" brings up all kinds of uncomfortable emotions and images.

Forget selling for a moment. But what about "serving"? Can we serve someone by selling them something that will make their life better? That's not so bad when you state it that way.

If you solve the problem, do an excellent job, and a happy customer walks away, you have served them well. If you feel that it was a task with no care or connection with the customer, you've lost the reason for doing business.

Serving your Who is the way forward in business. As consumers become more informed, they want to be served - not sold to.

Here's an example of how sales and service can work together: If you were a plumber and someone called you and asked, "Can you fix my toilet? There is a Barbie that got flushed, and nothing's getting through anymore" (With three young daughters, this scenario is not as much of a hypothetical in my life). A good plumber would never respond to the person in crisis, "Sorry, I don't do sales calls. They make me feel a bit too...you know... 'sales-y.'"

That would be ridiculous.

It would be in the inquirer's best interest if you sold them your service. Sell them on exactly how you could serve them, easing the stress and anxiety of a plumbing problem outside of their skillset.

Would the plumber who described what he did, how he did it, and how much he charged for being deemed a pushy salesperson? Not at all. It serves the potential customer well to tell them how you can solve their problem. People want to know how what you do can make their life better.

You Are A Servant, Not A Slave

Serving does not mean saying "Yes" to every request from every client. It doesn't mean being their slave either.

The two words, "servant" and "slave" can get mixed up. In fact, these two word come from the same Greek word, "doulos".[2] "Slave" and "servant" are connected in their etymology, but they do not have the same meaning in our contemporary vernacular. "Slave" is loaded with all kinds of abuses and horrific imagery.

In the name of serving others, we do not become their slave. We can let go of our desire to be served, in the interest of assisting another. But we always hold on to who we are when we enter someone's world. We all have a unique, powerful self that we bring into every relationship. We must never feel like we need to change who we are just because someone else wants us to be someone else to suit their needs.

What Does It Mean To Serve?

People mistakenly think that if I have to serve someone, I must be less valuable than them. Serving goes against the caricature we have in our heads about the characteristics of truly important people. They don't serve; they get served, right?

Being fed grapes all day while sitting on a throne is the ultimate dream. Well, not really.

If you had the choice of feeding the grapes or being fed them, you'd likely choose the latter. This image is not a realistic situation for most of us. If you're over two years old and are still being fed grapes, my point may not apply to you. Feel free to skip this section. For the rest of us, we need to see the power in serving others to be motivated to get up and show up every day ready to serve our customers and staff.

Faithful servants hold enormous power. They choose to give up their desire to be served so that someone else can benefit from their toil. In the twenty-first century, we have an abundance of case studies of historical leaders, inside and outside of business, who showed true greatness because they served others first.

Today, a servant doesn't mean we spend our lives washing floors and taking out the garbage (but it might be the case for some). Servanthood means when we choose to be selfish or self-centered, we humbly deny ourselves and work for the good of another. When someone does that enough times, others notice. They draw a crowd. Someone with a crowd gets our attention. We listen to them. We follow them. Their influence starts making things better. And history acknowledges this by calling people like this "great". Sometimes we take a national holiday in honor of them.

Their movement started with a motivation to serve other human beings.

The One Thing That Great Leaders Have In Common

Do you want to be a great business leader? It starts with a heart to serve. That's what Jim Collins noted as the distinguishing characteristic of the best leaders he surveyed.

In *Good To Great*, a must-read for anyone serious about excelling in business, Collins observes what all Level 5 leaders (the ones who lead at the highest levels) have in common. His findings surprised a lot of people.[3]

It's "humility".

Humility is the common denominator found in the most influential leaders at the front of the biggest companies. Who saw that one coming? A fascinating study, Collins surprised the business community in 2001 when his research came out. Most were expecting "powerful," "action-oriented," or "visionary" to top the list of these leaders. That wasn't it. It was humility that set them all apart. Humble leaders serve. That posture of the heart, that demonstration of "it's not about me" attitude, is what motivates people to follow them.

Alternatively, we've also heard about and witnessed terrible leaders who lived each day with a repulsive hubris they brought into every interaction. They were dreadful leaders because they only looked out for themselves. While a narcissist can use strategy to rise to power, their legacy will be tarnished. History never looks favorably upon those who commit their lives to being served.

So let's put away our cartoon ideas about what servanthood is and embrace the uncomfortable truth: Servanthood, humility, and greatness are tied together, especially if you want to be remembered well by history.

It's Tough To Be Humble With Jerks

We can sometimes mistake wanting to be humble with thinking we have to be like office carpet. Does being humble mean you just let people walk all over you all day?

It doesn't. Humble service of others does not mean any customer or client gets to dictate what you must do for them. Service is a choice. You get to decide how you will spend your time and energy.

You can say "No" to any client or customer and still be serving them. And it's OK to fire clients if it's the best course of action for everyone's betterment. Simply taking continuous disrespect or abuse from someone is not serving - it's enabling their poor behavior to continue.

You're probably thinking of a client right now that you could let go of. The relationship has become toxic. They're not treating you well. You are being disrespected. You despise emailing this client. You cringe when you see their number come up on your call display.

Yes, it's that person. You can let them go.

It's not worth whatever money they are giving you. They're capping your time and sucking your soul. They take up eighty percent of your time and do not compensate accordingly. You could be genuinely helping so many other people if they weren't holding you back.

Unhealthy people will try to take advantage of your kindness to them. They'll never be happy enough. Needy people will see that you have something to offer and try to suck it from you.

Don't let them. Your time, energy, and expertise are yours to give. They are not someone else's to take.

It could be that the most loving thing you do for them is to hold them accountable for their actions. Speaking the truth about what you have experienced becomes the challenging part of the soured relationship.

Doing that is the only way forward if your relationship with this client is going to go anywhere.

Professionals Always Show Up, Ready To Serve

Imagine visiting a local doctor and waiting in the waiting room for a few hours (commonplace in Canada). After it's finally your turn, he rants to you about the long day he has had, adding that that he is tired of seeing patients and only wants to go home.

Or what if you went to your mechanic and he confessed to you that he's going to do only the bare minimum to your car today. What he's looking forward to is checking out early to go golfing in the afternoon.

We expect professionals to show up and serve.

We expect professionals to be servants, even when they don't want to. Let me tell you a memorable story that showed me what servanthood looked like when I needed it badly.

The Servants Who Saved My Daughter's Life

When my youngest daughter, Gracie, was two, we had a terrible experience that forever jolted our hearts. During our medical crisis with Grace, I witnessed how true professionals performed in their service to others.

Gracie was a healthy, vibrant two-year-old girl. One day our toddler began to run a high fever. My wife was quick to act, taking all the necessary precautions that a great mom does. She took her to the doctor right away. During the appointment, Gracie's fever continued to spike. The doctor was unsure of what was wrong and recommended the usual Advil and rest to ride out the fever. Fifteen minutes later, Gracie became blue in the face. Her eyes rolled back and the two year old fainted in my wife's arms.

Hayley instinctively called 911. With trembling and fear in her voice, she quickly explained to the operator what was happening. Within minutes the an ambulance with two paramedics arrived. They gave Gracie a quick check. She was conscious, crying loudly and very uncomfortable because of her fever. She was put on a stretcher, and driven to the emergency room.

I arrived at the scene after following ambulances' sirens. I saw the stretcher with little Gracie come off the truck and ran to my wife who was chatting with paramedics. They immediately informed me on what was happening. Things had improved with Gracie under their care. I am forever grateful for those paramedics who showed leadership with empathy with everyone, especially us panicked parents.

As a parent, there is nothing more important to me in the world than my kids' health. The professionals were not only at the top of their game at the scene but they stuck around, providing extra care to all of us for whom this was a shocking first.

Thankfully, Gracie was ok. We had three days in the hospital running all kinds of tests on her. From what we were told, she just got hit with a nasty virus which triggered a major reaction in her little body. As I reflected on the events that unfolded on the day we called 9-1-1, I've always been impressed by how those paramedics treated us. They were true professionals. I've seen enough bad experiences from people doing the bare minimum at work. I know it could have been so much worse if they weren't on it.

Imagine if the paramedics were slow getting to the scene. They could have listed all kinds of excuses as to why it happened. They could have blamed the broken healthcare system. They could have moped about their dated trucks that they thought could use an upgrade.

What if the call came at the end of a long shift, and they were all "peopled out" that day? What if, knowing they were paid hourly, they took the long route to attend to the call, just to pad their timesheets a bit?

I can't fathom what would've happened if their dispatcher went off and they thought, "You know, we've been saving lives all day; we can afford to lose at least one today..."

I am certain these paramedics would never do that. Our first responders fight all day to save lives – every single one of them. Every call. They believe every life is important. No matter how they feel, they still know it's their job. They're not the only ones worth recognizing.

To The Champions Who Fought COVID On The Front Lines

Remember the overwhelming outpouring of support for front-line medical workers during the COVID-19 crisis? It was a well-deserved commendation for those who risked their lives to care for those who needed the highest levels of care during the pandemic.

These heroes went to work each day, exhausted from the days and weeks prior. They fought their fears of getting the virus. They even worked through waves of exhaustion, burn out and mental health challenges. They pushed back tears of the devastation from the virus and continued to serve, serve, serve.

They provided the face of what it meant to care during COVID.

One of the legacies of the COVID-19 crisis is how the medical community modelled to us what professionals do.

Why Your Job Is As Valuable As A Healthcare Worker

Relationships are vital to our success inside and outside of business.

Your work is likely different than those who fight for our health. In some ways, however, it's not different at all. At the end of every job, every project, and every gig is a person you're helping. They may not be fainting before coming to you, but they are still in some kind of distress. That's what led them to reach out to your company.

"It's just a video I'm creating for them," you might say.

What if that video isn't just a video? What if that's the video that is going to help their business connect with new customers by boosting engagement on their website and finally getting engagement on social media? They hired you because they had a major issue: They weren't connecting with the head and heart of their customers. They know that having a powerful video that tells a compelling story will help them reach new people. They need to reach new people because their business is currently failing. When their business is failing, their finances are a mess. They may have to let go of employees (who they also consider like family) whose livelihood depends on that business. To avoid layoffs, the business owner is having to work more. They're spending less time connecting with their family. Now the marriage is struggling because the owner is a bear to be around at home due to stress and anxiety.

What could end the downward cycle? Could the perfect video help? You bet it could. You already know the potential of your work unleashed into the market. You know what you can do for others. This project you're working on, if it's done well, could change everything for this business, these families, and the life of this owner who hired you.

Do you still think you're just creating a video for some random client? Not unlike those of us who depend on the care of our healthcare workers, your clients need you to be a professional and bring your best to every job.

What if you're not making anything for your customers? What if you feel like just a cog in some enormous wheel? If you feel like a dispensable part of an enormous system, consider how valuable the half a million Amazon employees are to us.

Jeff Bezos shared the impact of Amazon while he was taking a victory lap in his final letter to his shareholders. His April 2021 address revealed how Amazon is changing lives. He broke it down to them as follows:

 Customers complete 28% of purchases on Amazon in three minutes or less, and half of all purchases are finished in less than 15 minutes. Compare that to the typical shopping trip to a physical store – driving, parking, searching store aisles, waiting in the checkout line, finding your car, and driving home. Research suggests the typical physical store trip takes about an hour. If you assume that a typical Amazon purchase takes 15 minutes and that it saves you a couple of trips to a physical store a week, that's more than 75 hours a year saved.[4]

We all know that time is our most precious resource. Amazon argues that they as a company can save us over three days in extra time when we utilize their services. A company saving me that kind of time is incredibly valuable. With that gift, I can now spend more time with my family, doing recreational activities, or working to add more value to my clients.

If you work anywhere along the Amazon supply chain; in the warehouse or as a driver, you might not see yourself as a professional transformer of lives. But you are. You have a part to play in serving others. As an Amazon Prime member, I would not enjoy the freedom of time without your help. When you show up to work and fill our orders with speed and precision, you are taking our time-strapped lives and giving us a little more freedom.

So please don't say that your job isn't as important or second-rate to any other professional out there working hard today. We have just as much responsibility to show up and serve as our frontline healthcare workers do.

You're Here Because Of Others

On the evening of September 2, 2010, Steve Jobs sent an email to himself. The email, which has been published as part of a new online archive, offers a glimpse into the mind of the late Apple co-founder. In the email, Jobs reflected on the help he received from the work of others:

 I grow little of the food I eat, and of the little I do grow. I did not breed or perfect the seeds.

I do not make any of my own clothing.

I speak a language I did not invent or refine. I did not discover the mathematics I use.

I am protected by freedoms and laws I did not conceive of or legislate, and do not enforce or adjudicate.

I am moved by music I did not create myself.

When I needed medical attention, I was helpless to help myself survive.

I did not invent the transistor, the microprocessor, object oriented programming, or most of the tech-

nology I work with. I love and admire my species, living and dead, and am totally dependent on them for my life and well being.

Sent from my iPad[5]

Even the best rely on the help and service of others. Every day at work you're either benefiting from the fruit of someone else's work or you're sowing seeds that will become something someone else will appreciate.

Our work is meaningful when we have a Who in mind.

What Professionals Do

Professionals show up to work, they roll up their sleeves, and they serve.

No matter how far removed you are from their contact, remember that it's alway people you're helping. That customer with the problem you're solving is someone's child, spouse, parent, grandparent, or friend. No matter what industry we are in, caring for people as they deserve should be central to our job.

Even if your last three clients went amazingly well, client number four knows nothing about it. Your clients and customers hire you because they think you can solve their minor crisis. Even if it's a referral customer, they don't know how well you will serve them until you show up and do it.

This is not *just* for Customer Service. All of business is service. Sales is service. Leadership is service.

It takes hard work, but serving is what professionals do.

———————————————————

1. Edelman, Marian Wright. *The Measure of Our Success: A Letter to My Children & Yours*. Beacon Press: Boston, MA: May 1992.

2. I took four classes of Greek in my seminary training. I didn't think I would need it for writing this book until I needed to make this point.

3. Collins, J. C.. *Good to Great: Why some companies make the leap ... and others don't*. New York, NY: HarperBusiness, 2001.

4. You can read all of Bezos' inspiring letter at: https://www.aboutamazon. com/news/company-news/2020-letter-to-shareholders. Accessed April 2021.

5. Steve Jobs Archive. https://stevejobsarchive.com/ Accessed September 12, 2021

FIVE

Keep The End In Mind

 Before you start climbing the ladder of success, make sure it's leaning against the right building.

- Steven Covey

A good man died one August day. He was loved by family, friends, and people around his community.

Somebody scheduled the funeral service on a day the lead minister was out of town. The church secretary alerted the family that the young associate pastor would be in charge of proceedings instead. The family was assured that they'd be well-served under the leadership of the young pastor.

The younger replacement pastor had never done a service like this before. He learned a few things in school about how to conduct a service and graveside. But there's a big difference between head knowledge and life experience in any profession. The pastor was incredibly nervous, especially since the deceased was well-respected in the community. The service would receive a lot of attention. He wanted to do a great job. He worked on his message late into the night on the eve of the funeral. Before bed, he went through every step that would occur the following day, from the service to what he would say and do at the graveside.

He tossed and turned through the night. He finally did get some sleep but was so exhausted by morning that he slept through his alarm. Once he finally woke up, the pastor was late, missing the service entirely. He rushed to meet the family at the graveside but got stuck in traffic. Even worse, he got lost in the middle of a vast cemetery and had to drive around and around looking for the right grave.

Eventually, the stressed-out pastor slammed on the brakes near fresh a pile of dirt surrounded by grass. There were no crowds by the time he arrived. They had all gone back to a family member's home. Two city workers were left, leaning on their shovels, taking a break.

"This is the spot," he thought. "I'm late, but I'm not *too* late."

The young pastor was keen to honor the buried man by delivering a powerful sermon. The pastor gave it all he had. He held nothing back. He delivered an inspiring and provoking message.

Feeling good about himself, he closed his Bible, straightened his tie, and walked back to his car. The preacher drove away with a sense of satisfaction that he had redeemed his earlier mistakes.

Once the car was out of sight, the two city workers resumed their work. In silence, they had to process the bizarre scene that had unfolded before their eyes. After a few scoops and a long pause, the one worker looked at the other and remarked,

"What do you think *that* was all about?"

His partner responded, "Man, I've been burying septic tanks for twenty years now, and I've never seen anything like *that* before."

What I Learned About Life While Doing Funerals

While I never had an experience as the above, I've had to learn a lot about measuring a life well lived (or not) by officiating funeral services.

Since I was pastoring at one of the leading churches in my city, it was not uncommon for me to officiate the funeral services for people I had never met. My church often hosted services when the families were expecting big crowds. We had one of the largest buildings in town, and it was a service to the community we were more than happy to offer.

In such cases, having never met the deceased, I was thrust into their lives during a time of immense grief and loss. I will never forget the funeral service I facilitated for a well-known man in our community. His name was Dale.

Dale's family came to me while grieving Dale's passing. They were trying to get their heads around what they were going to do now that their patriarch was gone. The sixty-five-year-old was a pillar in their family. From everything I heard and saw, Dale was an amazing husband, dad, and grandpa.

While the extended family unit was enough to draw a crowd, Dale's years in the community as a small business owner were the reason for the larger venue.

It is a sacred moment to be there as people pass from one life to the next.

As we discussed arrangements for the service and went through the family's wishes, Dale's widow made an interesting comment.

"I hope we can fit everyone in the sanctuary."

That caught me off guard. Our main auditorium held 700 people. We even had video feeds available in an overflow room. Usually, that was more than enough space for a funeral. I was curious about this Dale guy who had the family questioning whether our facility would be large enough for his funeral.

If I was going to lead his service, I reasoned that I better get more acquainted with his story to avoid looking foolish.

I did what most millennials do when they have a question – I went to Google. With a quick search of Dale's name, a business listing was the first to pop up.

I learned Dale was a longstanding mechanic in town.

Having officiated funerals for over a decade, I had come to see these services as interesting but entirely predictable: Friends and family gathered together to celebrate the deceased. They go through a predictable liturgy with a reception that's capped off by the consumption of egg salad sandwiches.

There's nothing like honoring your loved one with egg salad between quarter-cut pieces of bread.

On the day of the service, I was keenly aware of who would show up. I noticed that most of the people in attendance were from Dale's work; they weren't only family and close friends.

I noticed something that stuck with me years later. Some of the most heartfelt, memorable, and responsive remarks on Dale's legacy came from people who were not directly related to him.

As a pastor, I was always intentional about spending time with guests at the reception after the funeral. It's not my love of egg salad that compelled me. I did this regardless of how well I knew the deceased person or their family and friends.

At Dale's reception, I kept getting stories from folks who Dale had impacted. Their comments further confirmed how much pride he always took in serving others at work.

It was evident that Dale went the extra mile with integrity to serve his customers every day. This was a refreshing characteristic from a man who worked in an industry tarnished by the dishonest and opportunity-seeking ones. Dale's memorial service was full of people who will miss him. That's because he personified what it means to care for and serve a Who.

The Kind Of Impact That Matters

Starting With Who is about making sure you impact people in your business so that they will feel compelled to attend your funeral.

It's not just a numbers game. We're not padding the stats of our final service to highlight our life's work, showing everyone we're important.

For a Why to be worth anything, it has to involve people. It's just a hobby if it isn't. Hobbies are great. But they don't have much lasting value or deep meaning to anyone but you.

As we learned last chapter, the outcome of a powerful Why involves impacting other lives in some way.

The Measure of a Successful Life

If you want to live a life of purpose and be known as someone successful, the question you need to ask yourself is:

How do you measure success?

Are there metrics we can use to determine if someone achieves real success?

Drawing a crowd these days doesn't impress me like it used to. With so much attention going online, it can be tempting to follow the dangling carrot of what is commonly called "Vanity Metrics."

Vanity Metrics are the online accolades expressed as follows, likes, shares, and retweets. It is easy to be deluded into thinking that getting the most vanity metrics is what measures success.

If you're trying to be the social media algorithm, those are the things that matter. But when you're running a business trying to reach people, they should not be the focus. I've seen companies with massive followings on social media get closed down almost overnight. They had a lot of "likes"; they didn't have much of a legacy.

What metrics do you use to determine a truly successful life?

It would help if you didn't build a business by making sacrifices and spending your time and money chasing vanity metrics only to see it vanish.

Work For Your Impact, Not Your Ego

A like or a share or a retweet is cool. It boosts algorithms and jolts egos, but it doesn't provide much when it's time to count what actually counts.

You shouldn't make vanity metrics your measure of success. How rewarding is it when a guy in his underwear gives you a thumbs-up on your post? Anybody with a grumpy cat or a cute baby can get likes and can go viral. A true impact is so much more than a flicker of attention.

My question is this: Can today's Influencer pack a room full of people who will vouch for the impact they made in the world?

Getting busy people to take time out of their crowded schedules to attend your funeral impresses me today. That's special. That's a sign of success.

That's what Dale had. I want it for you too. We need to care more about drawing the *right* kind of crowd, not just a big group. When everyone else is chasing vanity metrics as if they had any lasting value, let's go for impact instead.

During his life as a small-town mechanic, Dale knew what success looked like. His passing drew a crowd of his loyal customers that came to honor his life and work. They were in the middle of a busy week (who isn't?). They all found a way to clear their calendar so they could attend Dale's service.

You will never witness this during your lifetime, but attendance at your funeral is a metric of success.

The Life Of Significance And Meaning

Everyone wants to live a life of significance and meaning. I've been arguing that you can do this in your business by impacting real people by offering them solutions to problems that are holding them back.

One way we can know you are successful at doing this is by Who attends your funeral/memorial to celebrate your life.

How do we make this happen?

We can reverse engineer a successful life by looking at the end of it and working our way back. This approach involves asking:

"Who do you want to be at your funeral?"

I'm pretty sure that at your funeral, your family and most of your friends will be there. Even that cousin with the opposing political views you fought with at Thanksgiving will be there.

It's what families do. Memorials and funerals are the one "family event" with the unwritten rule of mandatory attendance. There are no excuses to miss this. I have heard numerous stories where the logistical challenges that family members have had to overcome to attend funerals. It's nothing short of miraculous.

Most of the family that attends will only take up the front two rows. Close friends might take up another row or two. What about the rest of the spots in the room? Who else do you want there? Whose life do you want to

touch so profoundly that when
your number is called, they will do
whatever it takes to attend your
funeral?

People go out of their way to come and celebrate your life.

Dale had friends, family, and
employees at his service. But the majority of people in attendance were his customers.

Our careers make up around one-third of our lives. The time we spend at work is one of our most significant opportunities to make a profound impact and difference in an individual's life.

One Word Of Clarification About Counting Heads At Funerals

We lost a lot of great people in 2020. Many lost their lives because of COVID, while others died of other causes during the outbreak. Regardless of how they passed, these precious lives never received the celebration they deserved. Funerals and memorials had to stay small and even virtual (if conducted at all) to slow the spread of COVID-19.

A year of anomalies and circumstances like this caution us that we must not take this point too literally. There are circumstances in which great people don't get a great turnout.

I'm not advocating for going to funerals and taking attendance to determine if someone was successful in business and life. The truth is that you could outlive all your customers. Imagine being a doctor, and you're so successful that all your healthy patients outlive you. That's a success if you ask me.

Or what if you're a grief counsellor and you're so good at your job that no one is devastated when you die? I wouldn't expect a huge following for a professional like that.

Or maybe someone cannot attend but would still like to. For example, if Dale had retired, moved to Arizona, and died there, his memorial service would only be a fraction of the size. None of his old customers would have heard of his passing and been able to celebrate and honor his life.

This hypothetical Arizona Dale would have been still just as successful as celebrity business owner Dale.

Filling up your funeral with people you have helped is a noble ideal and a helpful goal, even if it's not a feasible reality.

A Word From One Of My Most "Successful" Clients

During a lunch meeting with a client, after the usual pleasantries about the weather, sports, and some business chatter, I was given a powerful word of wisdom.

In passing, I mentioned the pressures I felt at the time. Each day was a grind trying to scale a business, raise a family right, and prioritize some of the ideas I had constantly going through my head. I got hit between the eyes with a word I knew was for my heart that day.

The wise sage I was with saw a young entrepreneur struggling with bigger dreams of growing a business. He paused, and, risking a cold lunch; he imparted some wisdom to me.

He explained,

 Jon, your ambition is honourable. But you'll one day find that the money doesn't matter at all. Once you make enough money to cover your bills, do a little investing, and pay for your three daughters' weddings, you're going to realize that just making more money isn't going to be enough... you need to find something bigger to live for.

It was a decisive moment. I knew it was true.

What would it profit to gain a world of wealth and lose all that truly mattered in the process?

He continued with the truth bombs, explaining how the rush of making money doesn't last. Eventually, you realize that money alone won't satisfy what your heart ultimately wants in life. We talked further about this, and then he offered one more thought. My client looked around the room, glanced out the window for a moment, and then leaned in. He explained in the tone of voice that evoked heartfelt wisdom, "At the end of it all, you want to know you achieved your purpose through your relationships."

I walked away from lunch that day with a full stomach and heart. Ambition is a powerful driver when it's taking us to the right place. Our ambitions should be centered around the right things - helping people.Our work should not just be about making more money. We get money for doing it, no doubt. Once you have enough to live, eat, drive a vehicle you own, and even go on a nice

When it's all over, your relationships are what count the most.

vacation, it's there has to be more. Chasing the money itself is an endless, frustrating pursuit with no natural finish line.

Life has to be more than money.

While we know this intellectually, how many of us remember it throughout the day?

If we followed you around this week, what would we conclude that you are living for? Is it the guise of monetary success or the achievement of genuine success - making people's lives better?

The Wasted Life

The famous Leadership coach John C. Maxwell quotes this poem in his book, *Developing the Leader Within You*:

> *There was a very cautious man*
> *Who never laughed or played*
> *He never risked, he never tried,*
> *He never sang or prayed.*
> *And when he one day passed away,*
> *His insurance was denied,*
> *For since he never really lived,*
> *They claimed he never really died.*[1]

This is the account of a life of missed opportunity.

It's the summary of someone who didn't seize the chance to impact others with his life at work. The man was protective of his heart, and he feared stepping out and taking risks. He probably didn't want to get his heartbroken. As a result, he kept his talents (and everything else) to himself.

He got one chance in life. He wasted it. Perhaps he never took the time to identify and overcome his fears. It could be that this man was too proud to serve others. Service, to him, was something people did for him. When his time was up, there was nobody around to testify about his impact on the world. He missed out. As the poem states, "he never really lived."

Suppose you are curious about what people are going to say at your funeral.

If you want to control what people say at your funeral (and make sure it's good), you will love this next exercise.

The Benefits Of Writing Your Own Eulogy

Have you ever thought about what people might say at your funeral service? Stephen Covey presented this idea in his famed self-help book, 7 *Habits of Highly Effective People.* Here's how he describes a now-famous exercise that highly effective people have been doing for years. Covey writes:

In your mind's eye, see yourself going to the funeral parlor, parking the car, and getting out. As you walk inside the building, you notice the flowers, the soft organ music. You see faces of friends and family you pass along the way. You feel the shared sorrow of losing, the joy of having known, that radiates from the hearts of the people there.

As you walk down to the front of the room and look inside the casket, you suddenly come face to face with yourself. This is your funeral, three years from today. All these people have come to honor you, to express feelings of love and appreciation for your life.[2]

As the scene unfolds, you realize that you are a guest at your funeral. You take a seat and watch the service begin. Four speakers will share stories about your life with all those present. While books and life coaches offer content about this subject, they focus only on what family and friends would say about you.

Here, I advocate for the consideration of how customers will eulogize you.

It's time to do some serious thinking. Some people work so hard to split their personal and work life. It's good to have healthy boundaries, of course. As people, we are not divided into distinct "work" and "home life" units. The relationships we make during our Monday to Friday careers are a significant part of your experience here on Earth. They are not to be downplayed as second-rate since they only happen at work. We are the sum of all our relationships since we are still the same person at work and at home (especially those who work from home).

We get the word "integrity" from the word "integer." It means the whole of anything. The opposite would be a fraction or a divide. A person lacks integrity when their life is divided in some way. No matter where we are or what we are doing, our whole lives are spent pursuing our Why. You know you've picked an important Why when it involves many Whos that you can impact.

Given that you spend so much of your time and energy at work serving customers, clients, or patients, what would you like one of them to say about you and the impact you made on their life?

Take a few moments to reflect on how you want customers to remember you. Write it down as best you can. Doing this exercise today allows the message to become ingrained in you.

You will find yourself with a new attitude and mindset that incorporates the thoughts, feelings, and benefits the customers will receive because of your newfound perspective.

Trying To Explain A Cemetery To Kids

We can't control when we go. But we can control what legacy we leave.

We can think we understand something until we have to explain that same concept to a kid. That's humbling. When I'm driving with my kids, we often pass by a cemetery. Without fail, my girls point to "the place where the dead people go." One day they were asking about the big rocks that were sticking out of the ground. I explained that the rocks are called "tombstones," and on the stones is information about who was buried there. Anyone with kids knows what is coming next...

More questions.

They asked what is written on the rocks. I guess for a kid, writing on rocks is usually silly pictures done with chalk. The writing I was talking about seemed different to their inquiring minds. I taught how on the rocks they wrote a name and some numbers. The first number is the year they were born. Then there's a dash. Then they put a second number which is the year they died.

More questions followed.

"Dad, what's a dash?"

Now that is a profound question. How do you describe what the little dash is about? The dash represents the life we lived. It tells the story of how we stewarded all those resources we consumed and the outcome of it all.

It reminds me of a powerful poem, fittingly called, *The Dash*:

I read of a man who stood to speak at the funeral of a friend. He referred to the dates on the tombstone from the beginning... to the end.
He noted that first came the date of birth and spoke of the

following date with tears, but he said what mattered most of all
was the dash between those years.
For that dash represents all the time they spent alive on earth and
now only those who loved them know what that little line is
worth. .
For it matters not, how much we own, the cars... the house... the
cash. What matters is how we live and love and how we spend
our dash.
So think about this long and hard; are there things you'd like to
change? For you never know how much time is left that still can
be rearranged.
To be less quick to anger and show appreciation more and love
the people in our lives like we've never loved before.
If we treat each other with respect and more often wear a smile...
remembering that this special dash might only last a little while.
So when your eulogy is being read, with your life's actions to
rehash, would you be proud of the things they say about how you
lived your dash?

Live Out A Dynamic Dash

The human mortality rate still hovers at around 100%. It always
has been that way. There are no exceptions.

Drink all the blended juice you want. Run all the marathons
you want. Eat all the fat-free dressing on your kale salad that
you want. Let the medical profession continue to be
enlightened.

We cannot control when our second number is called. We didn't get a say in our first number, for that matter. We can only decide what we will do with our dash. We get to choose what kind of legacy carries on after we're gone.

You can start living a better dash today.

The reality remains: you're going to die one day. Then they will have a service, and people will eat egg salad sandwiches while reminiscing about you.

What do you want them to say?

The Whos you serve today will be the ones who responsible for telling your story and living out your legacy tomorrow.

---

1. Maxwell, John. *Developing the Leader Within You*. HarperCollins Christian Publishing, 2018.
2. Steven Covey. *The Seven Habits Of Highly Effective People*.

SIX

Who Is Your Target And Your Market

 Make a customer, not a sale.

- Katherine Barchetti

L et me tell you why they call me "The Funny Morrison Brother." It's has nothing to do with humor.

It's more of a consolation prize since "The Successful Morrison Brother" was already taken. I don't mind getting the family equivalent of a participation trophy. It's what we Millennials do best. I'm proud of what my younger brother did in finding and serving his Who. If nothing else, it gave me a most fitting case study to learn from. It emphasizes the power of focussing on a Who.

The way my brother did it is an entrepreneurial success story that will encourage you. He was the founder of a software company that was sold privately after a decade of growth. His story tells of the rewards of regular people finding a Who and then serving that Who for years.

In 2009, Matt graduated at the top of his class at our local technical school. He finished his education, focusing on software as a service (or "SaaS" as commonly called). With the ink still drying on his certification, Matt started a web design company with the hopes of helping *any* company that needed a website and was willing to pay him. Like most entrepreneurs starting a business, he stumbled along at first. He managed to get a few clients here and there, charging whatever he could to pay bills and make it to the next job.

In those days, there were no "drag and drop" DIY website builders. When you created a website for a client, you had to build it from scratch.

Typical of most small business owners, Matt had huge dreams and yet struggled to make ends meet. He was willing to code a website from scratch for almost anyone.

Matt's fate changed when the tiny church he was attending asked if he would build them a website. This young church confessed to being on a shoe-string budget. Matt admits that he almost made nothing on that job. It was a labor of love for a cause he was passionate about.

This job was the seed that would lead to a harvest he had no idea was coming.

As Matt listened to his client's needs, he found out the staff had high needs but low technical ability. Knowing the new site would be managed by a volunteer, Matt made the website so easy to edit that even the most technologically inept receptionist could manage it.

Nobody was doing that at the time.

This website not only looked great and it worked so well. They started telling others. Matt's work generated a buzz. Soon a much bigger church in town wanted Matt to create their website. He

The lesson he was learning then was leading to a huge payout later.

noticed that the same features he spent hours coding for next to nothing for his church were precisely what the next church needed. He was able to get the site done quickly and even made a little money this time.

It didn't take long for Matt to get his third, fourth, and fifth deals. More and more churches wanted what Matt had done for the others. Matt made it simple for his Who to make changes on their site. His clients loved that they could take ownership of the content without having to do complex coding. Matt hired a team that worked on continually improving their processes. Their efficiency allowed them to work faster and offer better pricing. This combination was a win-win for both Matt and his Whos.

Matt discovered the treasure of knowing your niche. He would customize his platform to work exclusively for churches. Every aspect of his company focused on helping churches all over North America get outstanding websites.

Since he only had one type of customer, he always knew what was needed. A new feature that worked for one customer would surely work for all.

Matt developed a burden to help churches (so many with lousy or no websites at all) make an essential step into the online world so they could reach people. Soon Matt was getting stories in the local newspaper and even traveling internationally to speak to church leaders about the power of a strong online presence. He was invited as a guest on podcasts. He developed a reputation as "the guy" to talk to when your church needed a website.

Ten years after he created that first website for his home church, a prominent American company specializing in faith-based technology approached Matt. They gave him an acquisition offer that he could not refuse. The company was sold in every entrepreneur's ideal exit.

This story is a perfect example of the power of focusing on your Who. Before Matt had clarity on whom he could help the most, he fumbled along as a small business owner struggling to make ends meet.

Those early years were full of struggle being spread thin like jam over too much toast. When Matt understood the needs and pain points of churches, he could capitalize on a market that needed his help. He met the need and scaled his business.

That's why he is introduced at parties, Thanksgiving and Christmas as, "The Successful Morrison Brother".

Principle 1: Get Clear About Your Target

Start With Who is an approach to keeping certain people central to your business. This chapter extracts what I learned from watching Matt succeed once he discovered his Who.

A business built around a clearly defined Who gets specific about solving a problem: when this is done right, your business can lead and dominate a market.

Hall of Fame NFL coach Vince Lombardi is famous for starting a season with his team by taking them back to the game's fundamentals. Making sure everyone on the team was on the same page, Lombardi broke down all the complexities of football, making it simple again. At the start of one season, he took a game ball, put it in the center of the room and declared:

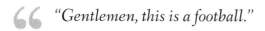 *"Gentlemen, this is a football."*

Lombardi coached some of the best football players in NFL history. Regardless of their experience and talent, he still felt compelled to make sure everyone was clear on what needed to be done to win.

If you simplify business to its elemental principles, where do you start? Put another way, "At its most basic level, what does a business need to succeed?"

The truth is, there are many things a new business needs to get going. Sometimes when I speak to crowds of entrepreneurs, I like to ask this question. The usual answers include these essentials for a business to succeed:

- a leader
- an idea
- some capital
- a lot of hard work

Still, there is one more core element that a business needs to truly be a business. Can you guess it?

It's customers. Every business needs customers.

It's as simple as pointing to the football in the middle of the room, right?

All Businesses Need Whos

You can't have a business without a Who. You need a customer

Those who try to reach everyone end up reaching no one.

paying for what you offer.

Who, then, should be *your customers?*

Can *everyone* be your customer? It's possible. But unless you're Amazon, it's highly unlikely. It's a waste of time trying.

If you try to reach everyone, you'll end up reaching no one.

Start With Who is about getting specific about whom you want to be your customer. Remember the Wandering Generality? A Wandering Generality has no focus, no commitment, and no impact.

Wandering generalities go from job to job and gig to gig. They never specialize. They're happy to turn over all the rocks on the surfaces and never dig down to find the genuine gold. Wandering Generalities never discover the impact they could have made.

When you're a generality, you also become a commodity. There's nothing special about being a commodity. As the saying goes, "generalists die poor." You're thrown in with all your competitors who do what you do and are willing to do it for cheaper. In a global marketplace, those people are easier to reach than ever. If you're trapped as a commodity, the only way out is to serve a Who/niche or charge less for what you do. The former is much more rewarding. "Who can charge the least?" is a race to bankruptcy.

If generalists die poor, the opposite adage is also true: *"The riches are in the niches."*

You Need to Be Specific

Seth Godin is one of our era's brilliant business minds, especially when it comes to providing the world with excellent, non-sleazy thoughts about marketing. With a gift for masterfully articulating common sense, Godin can even make marketing sound normal. In his book, *This Is Marketing: You Can't Be Seen Until You Learn to See*, Godin stresses the importance of getting clear on your Who. Every marketer needs clarity on who you are trying to reach whenever you talk about your idea:

 The most important lesson I can share about brand marketing is this: you definitely, certainly, and surely don't have enough time and money to build a brand for everyone. You can't. Don't try. Be specific. Be very specific.[1]

There are over seven and a half billion people in the world. It's growing all the time. Do you have to reach all of them? Of course not. There's no way you can learn that many languages. You know one language. You may learn a couple more. But you will never be able to speak to everyone around the world.

This limitation is incredibly liberating for you. Rather than thinking you have to reach the world, Starting With Who says that you only have to reach a tiny percentage of Earth's inhabitants to be successful.

Would you be happy if only .01% of the world's population became a customer? I bet you would be.

What if, among the seven and a half billion, there are ten thousand people you can help? That means there are ten thousand people who woke up today frustrated, stressed, and anxious because they have a problem they can't solve on their own? You can solve it for them.

Could you build a business with ten thousand people? I know many of the world's leading brands would love to have that many people, as long as they were the right ones.

What Can Be Done With 1000 True Fans

You don't even need ten thousand to have a comfortable living," argues Kevin Kelly, *Wired Magazine*'s founding editor. Initially published in 2008, Kevin Kelly's work reached a tipping point since his article "1000 True Fans" was included in Tim Ferris's bestselling book, *Tools of the Titans*.[2] I deem it essential reading for any budding freelancer looking to break into a market and grow a business. Let me give you a quick rundown of the article and why I believe it is so important. Kelly states:

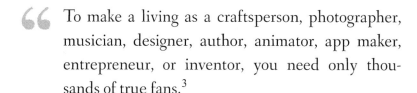 To make a living as a craftsperson, photographer, musician, designer, author, animator, app maker, entrepreneur, or inventor, you need only thousands of true fans.[3]

Not to be taken as a precise number, the article argues that you only need one thousand people to make a great living. That's one thousand souls who gobble up everything you put out.

These are the ones who love and value your work so much that they are more than happy to pay a premium to have it.

To accomplish this, Kelly recommends that you develop a close relationship with your customers. You know them. You know what they need. They know you as well. That's why they love you. With a thousand people as your benchmark, you can devote your time to providing these *Superfans* with the best experience possible.[4]

I'm convinced that these days if you have a brain, a heart, and the drive to show up consistently, you can lead a group of people who will join you on your mission to fulfill your Why.

Here's the truth: If you try to be everything to everyone, you will matter very little to many people. But if you focus on a small tribe of people, you can significantly impact them.

The Power of Tribes

Since the dawn of humanity, people have gathered into tribes. Tribes are built around ideas, cultures, geography, family connections, hobbies, and anything else that draws people together.

Years ago, Seth Godin identified the Internet as a catalyst to community. The Internet allows people who would've otherwise been unconnected to rally together as a tribe. Today, with the help of social media, you can find a tribe for pretty much any interest.

In *We Are All Weird - The Rise of Tribes and the End of*

Normal, Godin argues that our modern world has allowed any subculture to gather. This gathering forms a community. These communities have their own cultures and markets. We know them as the Cross-Fitters, Warlocks, Beliebers, Swifties, Keto-crazies, Paleos, or the Facebook group devoted to rallying the "People Who Go Out Of Their Way To Step On A Crunchy Leaf".

The Internet has allowed us to find each other and connect in meaningful (and bizarre) ways. I encourage the former and accept the latter.

Start With Who means finding the tribe you know you can connect with and serve the best.

The Internet has allowed us to connect to each other in meaningful (and bizarre) ways.

Lonely Calculus Teachers
No More

In the past, if you were a calculus teacher and you wanted to connect with and share ideas with other calculus teachers, what would you do? How would you find people like you? You don't usually bump into them when you're hanging out at a coffee shop or the grocery store.

In the past, if you wanted to lead a mastermind for calculus teachers, how did you find other people who shared that area of interest with you? Put up a poster in the local library? Or maybe slap an announcement on the door of the movie rental store? You could write and mail a letter to all the high schools inviting the teachers. All these methods would take time and would be futile to try. So calculus teachers would've sat there alone, keeping their ideas to themselves.

Today, on the other hand, if you want to find another calculus teacher and form a group, you can go online and ask if there's any out there. Right away, people will come out of nowhere and raise their hands. People are doing this right now. There are calculus networking groups, online calculus tutoring available, and *How to Teach Calculus* courses you can take online from anywhere around the world. And it's not calculus teachers who have a monopoly on getting connected. It's like that for *every single part of our society*.

It's never been a better time to find your tribe.

When it's Time to Hunt

Suppose you're a hunter, and you've got a ticket to hunt moose. In that case, the hunting experts, government regulators, common sense, and Wikipedia articles don't encourage you to show up with a shotgun and start firing at everything in the forest. The successful hunter finds out where the moose hang out and then goes there. I have an uncle who loves to hunt. He tells me that hunting any animal has its unique challenges. You can't just stroll into the bush and take a shot.

If you want to lure a moose, you not only need to know where they are, you also need to know their movement patterns.

Every animal is different. A hunter knows it's worth the time to study the traits of each animal while learning what tactics other hunters use to achieve success.

When you put all the pieces in place and use your tactics and tools correctly, the right animals will show up.

The analogy transfers into the business world seamlessly.

Too many businesses get dressed up in hunting regalia and try to hunt every animal in the forest. They have no clarity on whom they are trying to reach, so they show up and open up their shotgun on the open market. They throw good money at social media and Google Ads that don't work. They spend countless thousands on a website that doesn't perform. They turn over their marketing department. Then they turn them over again.

They try talking to everyone. Aiming at everyone leads to hitting no one.

You Need a Tribe

Without a tribe (what we call "Your Who"), you'll be another voice shouting into the noisy abyss.

Our world doesn't need any more noise. One entrepreneur or even a giant enterprise can't reach everybody. Some consumers prefer the personal treatment of a mom and pop. Others like the convenience of an enterprise. The good news is that the pie is big enough for everyone.

The *Start With Who* principles offered thus far highlight the importance of having a target to direct your attention to. Where do you aim without a target? No wonder so many businesses waste so much time with random acts of marketing that don't do anything for them.

If you're not connected to a tribe, you'll be a voice shouting into the abyss.

Not so when you have a clearly defined Who.

Principle #2: State The Problem To Seize The Market

Your tribe has a problem that keeps them up at night. When they finally do get to sleep, the problem is sitting there at the edge of their bed, welcoming them first thing in the morning. All day long, it has them on a treadmill of despair and angst.

Whatever the case may be, they are stressed out, frustrated, and anxious. Each day they're losing a little more hope that someday things will be better.

They're looking for someone to help.

While you can't solve *all* their problems, you and your company can solve one or two of them. You'll use your product, service, a course you create, or whatever it is you've been working on to help them.

The powerful thing about business is how it revolves around this premise: we all have problems, and we all need solutions for them. The bigger the problem you can solve, the more money your Who will be willing to invest in getting the solution from you.

Someone in pain without a clear solution is what creates a market. Businesses come in and, in exchange for money, help them overcome the problem.

> Your clients would be happy to discuss their pain points. You have to care enough to ask them.

How Well Do You Know Your Who's Problems?

When you know your Who well enough, you'll be aware of their pain points. If you don't know the pain, you're not listening closely enough. People love talking about their problems. They will leave reviews, comments and flat out tell you over a cup of coffee what is bothering them.

Most people are happy to chat about their frustrations when you ask them.

You have to be listening for it.

The reason we don't do this is because it takes time. Frankly, it's easier to get together with colleagues and speculate about what we *think* the problem might be.

Of course, when you do this, you're at risk of missing the actual customer's pain point.

If there is no pain point, there is no opportunity. If people don't find value and a solution to their pain, they will not surrender their hard-earned money in the sale.

It seems too obvious to use up all this time talking about. However, I've seen too many entrepreneurs think they have a brilliant idea that we all know won't work - except the blind-spotted entrepreneur, of course. Without a clear Who with a pain point, there's no market for their idea.

Again, Seth Godin summarizes it well:

 It doesn't make any sense to make a key and then run around looking for a lock to open. The only productive solution is to find a lock and then fashion a key. It's easier to make products and services for the customers you seek to serve than it is to find customers for your products and services.[5]

Starting With Who, helps you discover the type of lock that's out there in the market. You'll know this because you'll be in close contact with your Who. Your expertise helps you make the key that fits the situation perfectly. Without a Who, you are just a key maker with a garage full of keys that nobody wants.

Life is too precious to spend it creating something that nobody wants.

Is Your Business Disruption-Proof?

One other significant benefit to staying close to your Who's pain points is that it protects you from the dreaded threat of disruption.

No one wants to face the same fate as Blockbuster, cab drivers, Kodak, or your (former) favorite neighborhood book store.

I think the ghost of these companies haunts business leaders. It torments them with the thought that the same fate is inevitable when the grim reaper of disruption knocks on their door.

Disruption is expected as the world keeps moving. Disruption keeps the business world fresh. Without disruption, systems and routines would get stale.

Disruption doesn't care about you. Disruption doesn't have feelings.

But disruption has no feelings.

It doesn't honor the past. It doesn't care about your employees or how you're going to feed your family. Even as you are reading right now, you can rest assured that disruptors are working late and rising early. Somewhere out there is an entrepreneur with a dream and a fire in their belly to disrupt you. They want to unsettle that comfortable system people in your industry have all worked so long and hard to enjoy.

That's ok. She's going to make you better. That's business. It's an adventure. Disruption keeps us on the edge of our seats.

Are you prepared for disruption?

How do you stop the invisible tide of disruption from wiping out your company? You guessed it:

You Start With Who.

Are You More Like Blockbuster Or Netflix?

Some readers will not remember when it was an "outing" to go to the video store. One of my favorite family activities growing up was going down with my parents and brother to begin the quest to find the perfect movie to watch that night. We had hopes that the new release we wanted would be available. At the video store, you could see groups of friends walking the aisles, searching for the perfect evening entertainment. Laughter could be heard around the room as famous lines from classic films were recited - or even whole scenes reenacted right there for all to see.

The video store was also a helpful place to get a recommendation from an employee. This person was always the community's envy. Their job was to sit around and watch movies all day. The employee was the guru of entertainment. They had seen every possible movie. They had the admiration of every teenager in town. Watching movies was *their job*. If it was a choice between *Movie A* and *Movie B*, the employee held the power to choose how everyone would be spending their time that night - what influence!

For my entire childhood, Blockbuster dominated the movie rental market. Families, couples, and friends flocked to the movie rental giant every night to catch a new release or see their old favorite for the hundredth time.

How could this experience ever be disrupted? People love consuming movies – but how much would they enjoy the experience of having to leave the house to get it? That was the question nobody asked until RedBox came around.

I remember when RedBox first arrived. Their big red boxes were found only at the front of grocery stores. It was a movie vending machine. You could rent a DVD from the box and then drop it off at the same place a few days later. Renting movies was no longer an event. It became purely transactional. Put your credit card in, pick your movie, grab the DVD, and go home.

Business lore tells the story that the Blockbuster board of directors was confronted with evolving technology and the rise of competitors like RedBox and Netflix. They had a difficult decision to make when they saw the disruption in their industry. Would they pivot to meet their customers' needs and desires or maintain the status quo, hoping the video store renter culture would be a bastion of suburban culture?

The board leveraged some data they found that assured them how much people enjoy going to the movie store. They assumed that the public would never give up the group rental experience.

My hunch is that Blockbuster found a consultant who told them that the best decision was coincidentally the easiest decision. They took the counsel to continue to do what they had always been doing. When you have an agenda, you can make a report look any way you want. Blockbuster even had the opportunity to purchase a young Netflix for a great deal at one point.

When Tough Decisions Need To Be Made

Netflix saw technology changing and was there to meet the convenience needs of the consumer. People discovered simpler ways to watch movies and binge-watch their shows. Netflix had followed Redbox for some time but soon ditched their vending machines at grocery stores. They went "all-in" with Internet streaming. They avoided disruption because of their commitment to their Who. They rejected the easy way out, the status quo, or even "what we are good at."

Blockbuster lost touch with its Who and is out of business. People are only talking about them as a case study in "What Not To Do." They will be a case study in disruption for decades to come.

How To Become A Disruption-Proof Company

Wouldn't it be nice to know that no matter how fast the world spins or how quickly technology changes, there will always be a source of income for you?

Would you like to have the peace of mind that comes from knowing when disruption comes for your business, you never have to worry?

There are a lot of scared business leaders out there today. I meet with many clients who have a deep underlying fear that they could lose everything to disruption one day. I understand why it freaks them out. Disruption has no compassion nor any obligation to you. It doesn't care at all about what you've done in the past.

Avoid disruption by staying in touch with actual customers.

If you have loyal customers, however, that changes everything. When you are close to your Who and serving them faithfully, they will care about you. When you are helping your customers win, they will stay loyal to you. You can evolve with them. That's how you avoid disruption - you stay connected to your customers.

Blockbuster and Netflix both watched technology disrupt how the public consumes entertainment. Only one has survived, and I believe it's because of Netflix's commitment to their Who.

They stayed close to the customer and kept in step with them along the way.

Disruption Is Coming

Eventually, every industry is disrupted by new ideas and technology. One thing that will never change is the Who. Some Who will always be part of the equation. Humans will still need help with something. Deep down, we all want to be more efficient, productive, attractive, healthy, smart, have more money, or all of the above.

Because no one can achieve all these on their own, we will always need help.

This world will always be broken. Human beings will always have sleepless nights worrying about something.

It's your job as a business person to find out what that something is and help them deal with it. Do that every day, and there will always be work and money to be made. The world doesn't owe you or your company anything. It's your job to show up and help people solve their problems so that you can help make their lives better.

As long as people are inhabiting the planet, there will be an opportunity to provide solutions for your Whos. That's where the market is.

How insulated are you from disruption? Forget about the competitor down the street. Is there somebody on the other end of the world that could put you out of business? Is there a technology that could make your job obsolete overnight?

To protect yourself from this, you need to be in close communication with your Whos. As you listen to what's bugging them, you can help them adapt. That way, you will always be scratching where the market is itching.

Is there somebody working hard today whose idea could put you out of business?

That's how Starting with Who helps you disruption-proof your business.

Case Study: How A Bunch of Chiropractors Became My Whos

I'm writing this chapter from an airport in Florida where I just finished speaking at a chiropractor conference in the area.

This event was my fourth big chiropractor event in the past four months. Over the past years, I've grown to love these chiropractors. I confess they were never on my radar for having as a Who. However, I'm humbled to say now that they are some of my favorite people to serve. How they became my Whos is a story worth telling.

This book was inspired by my years of experience as a Story-Brand Guide. I worked with the author, Donald Miller, and his team to help businesses create clear marketing messages and collateral connected with a company's ideal client.

In the same year that I started with StoryBrand, Facebook's Mark Zuckerberg announced that Facebook would be boosting one of its features, *Facebook Groups*. Facebook's stated goal was to make social media social again. It's not often that the famous Facebook CEO gives us a clear direction of what direction the company is heading. I knew these groups were going to be a significant thing for a long time on Facebook. I was always the opportunist; I created a Facebook group for those who wanted to talk about StoryBrand. At this point, I had no Who - just a topic I could help people with.

As enrolments started to come, I began helping any business owner who asked about marketing and messaging. I gave out hours of free help. We worked together on improving their company tagline, crafting elevator pitches, and fine-tuning the words on their website.

One of the first members to join the group was a chiropractor from Colorado. He asked many provoking questions about how he could create a clear message for his patients. He and I had conversations about how chiropractors can connect with their target demographic. After all, as a part-time athlete who likes to think he can function as a full-time one still, I have spent more than my fair share of times at the chiropractor (the plight of an aging hockey player).

Not long after our exchange, I was invited to a Zoom call to speak with a mastermind group with ten other chiropractors.

My host briefed me beforehand about what to expect. I learned that the topic they would be covering that day was "branding and brand messaging." I just had to show up and talk about that.

I shared an abbreviated presentation on the power of clear brand messaging. I wasn't prepared for what happened next. One doctor asked me to tell him what I thought of his website. I tried to be a polite Canadian but still let him know that it was terrible.

For the next hour, I dissected and gave feedback on what was lacking on several of the chiropractor's websites. I thought it would lead to the end of my time with them. In Canada, you see, that's how we lose friends. When you're mean to someone about their website, you stop getting invited to parties.

Much to my surprise, the chiropractors all received my feedback gracefully and with open minds. The meeting went so long, it made me late for dinner.

After my commute from work (across the house from my home office to the dinner table), the family sat down for dinner. My wife inquired about the meeting. "It was fine," I replied, more interested in eating and helping the kids get fed than discussing the international diplomacy mess I had made.

 "I think I just pissed off a lot of American chiropractors, though."

We thought nothing of it and went on with dinner as usual.

The following day, my email had a bunch of invitations from

the chiropractors who were on the call. I was unaware that these guys were some of the leading young chiropractors in America, each with enormous online followings. One had a marketing podcast of over 3,000 listeners. Another was the administrator of a Facebook Group of over 8,000 chiropractors. He also had a podcast. I accepted every invitation to be a guest and do podcast interviews. The listeners must have taken what I said to heart. The inquiries started coming from doctors all over the continent. One thing is for sure; it confirmed the power of masterminds!

In just a few short months, I had my plate full of work coming in from chiropractors around North America. Working with them was satisfying. We share a joint commitment and value to care for people. They were adamant early on that they were a subculture of chiropractic with the opportunity to change the profession. They cared about being led by the best scientific evidence, not what gave them the most profit.

These doctors valued giving patients extra care when needed, not seeing them as numbers or files.

They also told me the importance of collaborating with other medical professionals and not being an island of chiropractic unto itself.

I liked that vision. I wanted the men and women who were working hard to make it happen. I believed in them. I found a way to help them. Now I'm wearing their badge.

That was important for me to know because my passion is to help reputable businesses grow. There's no point putting my time and energy into a company that will do more harm than good.

Because of the growth of my business, business owners in different niches began to contact me. I learned that some of these industries were hard to work with. Many did not align with my thoughts, beliefs, and values. Because I already had more than enough work from a group I enjoyed working with, I now had the freedom to say "No" to groups with whom I didn't connect.

The chiropractors were educated, humble, and respectful people. Knowing the commitment it would take to help this subculture of the medical profession advance (their Why), I made it a point to show up both in the online groups and at their live events.

As we connected, I paid close attention to what was bothering them about marketing and websites. These were the pain points that jumped out to me. While it was their job to help people get out of physical pain, I could ease the pain of losing patients and not growing their practice because of lousy marketing.

These chiropractors were top-notch when treating patients, but they seemed to struggle to communicate what they could do with simple words. They needed help to create a compelling message connected to both head and heart of the people they could help. I set to work tailoring products and services that could help them get clear marketing. As mentioned above, most of their websites were terrible. It was my job to do the most loving thing and point it out. It's cruel to remain silent when someone is talking to you with salad in their teeth.

We have to speak the truth. We have to speak the truth infused with and motivated by love.

I identified two problems I knew I could solve for these chiropractors:

1. How to create a clear message that connects with their ideal patient.
2. How to create a winning website that they'd love and would engage their ideal patient.

That's all—just those two things. For the next few years, I showed up, stayed in my lane, and helped solve those two problems. Let me tell you that it's a lot easier to teach marketing to a chiropractor than to teach chiropractic to marketers.

With clear focus, we have now helped thousands of chiropractors all around the world.

Finding my groove was a work in progress. There were times I was charging too much. There were times when I was charging too little. I had some excellent ideas. I had many bad ones. There were times when I would create something that didn't connect. Thankfully, my Whos were honest, providing excellent feedback to make me more useful.

One day I realized I had became known in one subculture of the profession as "the guy you call when you need a website that will work for you."

My heart grew for those in this unique medical profession. Unlike dentists or surgeons, the margins for making it as a chiropractor are slim. I have become a bleeding heart who wants to help them not just get by but also thrive in their practice.

That's why I travel around North America, speaking at conferences for chiropractors. Friends and family laugh when I tell them this. I would have never guessed this would happen when I started that Facebook group.

You Start to Love Your Who

I'm not using this story to flaunt pseudo-celebrity stories of exotic travel. There's not much exotic about St. Louis, New Jersey, and Toronto (though Florida in December was lovely, I admit). I'm sharing this story to encourage you how quickly things can change when you find a group of people you can help.

I never dreamed about how my life could be changed by accepting an invitation to speak with a few chiropractors. They've since invited me into their family.

Are you struggling to find a Who of your own?

Be encouraged. Breakthrough could happen any time.

If you've felt the consequences of being a wandering generality, remember this: In just a few months, somebody could welcome you into a network of Whos. In no time, you'll be showing up, adding value, and being invited to come back and do it again.

I've made life-long friends with my clients. With their own hard-earned money they have grown my business, helped me employ other people, and grown the economy.

One of the real joys I get out of serving my Who is the regular stream of emails, Google reviews, and raving social media posts from satisfied clients. I love reading how our team's work on their websites has helped them gain new patients.

What I love the most is knowing the stories behind those rave reviews. That, to me, is worth so much more.

I'm so glad I started that Facebook group several years ago. It led me to a clear target that I could get to know and love. It opened my eyes to a market that I could serve. What I didn't see coming is the joy I would get in the process. I have received tremendous joy in discovering and serving my Who. I didn't expect this. I wake up each day with a sense of duty and purpose. It's my job to work hard to impact people who are working hard to help other people.

I'm hoping that one day, a handful of them will jump in a plane to attend my memorial one day.

Who Are Your People?

This chapter taught us how you get a guaranteed target and a market when you Start With Who.

These are two essentials for any

successful business, right from the startup to the established enterprise. Every business needs a customer. Having a clear Who, knowing their pain points, and solving their problem is how you can know your business will have what it needs to grow and thrive for years to come.

Serving a niche makes your work more focused, fruitful, and financially rewarding.

Do you have a story similar to Matt's success with churches or my journey with chiropractors? I'd encourage you to start thinking about it. Is there a particular group to whom you feel drawn? Have you had success helping a specific demographic?

In the following chapters, you will clarify your thinking as you answer these questions and get clear about your Who.

It's worth it. It makes your work more focused, fruitful, and financially rewarding.

---

1. Seth Godin, *This Is Marketing: You Can't Be Seen Until You Learn to See.*
2. Ferriss, T. *Tools of titans: The tactics, routines, and habits of billionaires, icons, and world-class performers.* United States: Billionaire Mind Publishing, 2017.
3. You can find Kelly's article in full here: https://kk.org/thetechnium/1000-true-fans/ Accessed April 15, 2021.
4. I highly recommend Pat Flynn's treatment of this subject as well. See Flynn, P. *Superfans: The easy way to stand out, grow your tribe, and build a successful business.* San Diego: Get Smart Books, 2019.
5. Seth Godin, This is Marketing: You Can't Be Seen Until You Learn To See.

SEVEN

Three Benefits To Getting Clear On Your Who

 Customer service is the new marketing.

-Derek Sivers

I n 2019, Chip Wilson released the book *Little Black Stretchy Pants: The Unauthorized Story Of Lululemon.*[1] This book chronicled Chip Wilson's humble beginnings as he built the now internationally recognized clothing line, *lululemon*. Wilson's story inspires me. He spotted an opportunity in the market that helped him serve a clear Who.

Let me tell you the back story, as recounted in Wilson's book.

Chip Wilson graduated from university in 1979. Wilson witnessed how the fastest-growing demographic graduating from university were young women. An opportunist and entrepreneur at heart, Chip Wilson saw that society was flooding the business world with single, professional women. These women were well educated, media-savvy, well-traveled, stylish, and active.

Furthermore, these women had the financial means to be well-dressed at all times, even while sweating it up at yoga.

Wilson took one of the first offered yoga classes and surmised an opportunity to outfit this subculture. To learn more about the women who took yoga and learn about this marketplace, he formed creative focus groups. Chip Wilson struck up conversations with attendees and instructors to learn about their primary pain points (related to what women wore at yoga).

Those old enough to remember what athletic apparel was like in the nineties will remember when men only wore baggy shorts and old t-shirts to the gym. Being used as gym clothes was the final phase in men's garments' life cycle before their wives threw them out. Women wore dance clothes or unflattering grey sweatpants to yoga classes. Clothes would chaff, stink and never fit right.

There was nobody doing anything to combine fashion and function. From his upbringing with a family who understood style, Chip knew a thing or two about sewing. He even knew how to source material and production from overseas.

> lululemon became a global brand because Chip Wilson obsessed with helping his Who.

Wilson and his growing team designed material that you could wear to work and then walk down the street and wear to the gym or a yoga class. It was the first time that a synthetic fabric felt like cotton. All of a sudden wearing gym clothes in public was a thing.

A new category of clothing was taking shape: *athleisure*.

Lululemon became a global brand because Wilson obsessed with helping a Who.

This chapter highlights what it means to be customer-centric. We look at how lululemon began with a clear focus to help a specific kind of consumer. Meeting the needs of a particular consumer was all Wilson cared about. Lululemon wasn't established out of self-service or chasing competitors. Wilson knew exactly who he could help. Then he helped them. And the world loved it.

No Growth Without Struggle

As any entrepreneur knows, growth does not happen without roadblocks and obstacles.

Wilson encountered his obstacles when the media, searching for a story to stir the pot, accused the outspoken Wilson of making fun of heavy-set women who wore his clothes.

In *Little Black Stretchy Pants*, Wilson explains what he meant when he said that his pants were not intended for everyone. Wilson was trying to argue to the hyper-sensitive media that his stretchy yoga pants were not to be worn like the other fashion phenomenon of the time, Spanx. Spanx was designed to be stretched to give its wearers the appearance of being smaller.

Not so with lululemon.

Its fabrics were not designed to be worn two sizes smaller than appropriate. That was Wilson's point. Throughout the book, it's clear that Wilson loves his target audience. I am confident that he would never resort to slandering his customers, as the media have suggested. I give him the full benefit of the doubt here. It's not the first time the media has taken something out of context to spin a story.

Chip Wilson was driven by his passion for helping a particular type of person. Lululemon never lost its passion for helping women have fashionable and functional clothing. It led them forward from their early days as a startup to becoming a globally recognized brand today.

Men and women want to feel good in their clothes.

In this chapter, you'll learn why your business needs to be driven to help people win. Any other motivation simply won't work.

Are You Driven To Help?

There are three motivators that drive companies. Only one of them gives the assurance of long-term success. I encourage you to think not about *what the right answer is*, but about what is really motivating *your* company. The three motivators are:

1. Self-preservation
2. Chase the competition
3. Help customers win

Let's break down all three and identify what category of motivation you are currently using so you can make adjustments accordingly.

Motivation #1: Self-Preservation

The first motivator driving companies is the need to take care of themselves.

On Maslow's famous hierarchy of needs, these companies are stuck at the bottom. They exist only to have their needs met in order to survive.

A company that is motivated by self-preservation concentrates its energy and attention on taking care of the company. This motivation must be shared by employees as well.

Every day, employees at all levels of the company show up to keep the company alive another day. Everyone has the goal of paying the invoices, meeting payroll, and keeping shareholders happy. Companies motivated by self-preservation work tirelessly to take care of themselves.

The trouble with the first motivator is its commitment to itself. If an individual took on these attributes, we call them "selfish," "self-centered," or worse. We don't like people like that. We don't want companies like that either.

When you visit an electronics or furniture store, you can quickly tell their employees' pay structure. A commission salesperson looks at you and talks to you differently. You can usually smell them before any of the other senses kick in. I'm not talking about physical smell, of course.

When someone is only looking to get a sale from you, they get what we call "commission breath." You know what commission breath smells like, right? The salesperson can't hide the fact that he or she only cares about you if they get some money from you.

When this happens, we intuitively back away and go somewhere else. Instinctively, humans are repulsed by self-centredness and self-interest. We can handle it in ourselves, of course, but we don't like seeing it in others – or the companies with whom we do business.

You can always tell when a salesperson sees you as just a big dollar sign.

It doesn't take long for customers to discover that an entire company is just looking out for itself. When everyone has a commission breath, a company stinks. When this is the case, the customer service is less than desirable. Because customers are more aware and have more power today than in any previous era, the company driven by self-preservation will be in trouble.

Motivator #2 - Chasing The Competition

The second motivator driving companies is keeping up with the competition. These companies watch what their competition is doing and copy them. The mantra for this type of company is, "If it's working for them, it should work for us as well."

Competition is the foundation of a healthy economy. It is often the catalyst for business growth. But too many companies spend all their time and energy trying to chase the competition. They obsess about visiting their competition's website (and they get there by draining the competitor's marketing budget by clicking the Google Ad!) and trying to see what they're doing.

Companies whose primary motivation is chasing the competition believe innovation is simply copying what their competitors are doing. The cusp of creativity is driven by trying to do it differently just enough not to get sued. Leaders in the company are often heard saying,

 "I hear that (competitor) is doing (something new). We should seriously consider this idea as well."

Chasing competitors may inspire some excitement early on. Still, it will not sustain consistent growth and success in the long run.

Do you want the copycat strategy to be your legacy? Just because your competitors thought of an idea first doesn't mean it's a good one. You can chase a company right into bankruptcy. This approach is also a morale sucker for your team.

No one wants to work for a company that only copies ideas from others. It sucks the creativity right out of your organization. It makes employees feel phony. And finally, because it doesn't Start With Who, it gets you out of touch with your actual customers.

Beware of chasing competitors. They may be headed off a cliff.

The blind can indeed lead the blind. The blind can lead the blind off a cliff or into market irrelevance. Neither are all that appealing.

There's a better motivator than putting yourself first and chasing the competitors.

Motivation #3 - Help Customers Win

The third motivator driving companies is this: *Help customers improve their lives by solving problems they're facing.*

Put more simply: *Help people win.*

They want to win in life, in business, in their relationships, and their health. Helping people win is another way to engage the "Start With Who" approach. Companies in this third category understand that their businesses exist to serve people.

They work hard to understand what serves customers best – doing everything they can to provide a great customer experience.

Amazon is a company known for getting a myriad of products from your phone to your door quickly. What has driven them to be one of the world's biggest companies is not their technology or warehouse space - it's customer service.

All through the company, there is a hardwired core value to keep customers first. One method that Amazon has implemented to make sure this is the case is to require managers to spend time answering phones at their call centers. Even Jeff Bezos, the CEO, spends two days each year in the call center. He talks to Amazon customers. This investment of time is there to ensure that those in charge of leading Amazon's team are in tune with Amazon's Who. It is evident Bezos believes the managers should stay focused on their customer-centric values and not lose touch with the heartbeat of the customers.

Bezos has proclaimed many times: "We're not competitor-obsessed, we're customer-obsessed. We start with what the customer needs and then work backward."[2]

He ensures this happens at every level of the company by keeping his leaders close to customers. By doing this, Bezos is assured that the Who of Amazon will be well served, so they will continue to pour billions of dollars through his company.

That's what Start With Who is all about.

It's Never Too Late To Shift

In his book *This I Know: Marketing Lessons From Under The Influence*[3], Terry O'Reilly tells a memorable story of how the leaders of the *Metro*, the Parisian transit company, discovered that an internal change in motivation could turn around the public's perception of their company.

Ridership was slumping as Parisians and tourists alike chose above-ground forms of transportation rather than their juggernaut of a subway system. As revenue declined, something had to change. The thing to change first, notes O'Reilly, was what motivated the Metro staff.

For years the company existed to appease its executives and shareholders. The consequences of this were a poor rider experience, and the Metro became inconvenient and eventually became irrelevant to the public it was attempting to serve.

The leadership of the Metro got a wake-up call and had to see people differently. No longer would the public be seen as a means to a bonus. Executives had to start valuing people again.

The Metro existed because people needed to get around comfortably and on time. The Metro leadership created a company policy to reflect their change of heart. They stopped calling people "Riders." Instead, they opted to call them "Customers." Riders were commodities. Customers were paid guests.

That's a big difference in perception. The more you understand French culture, the more you will appreciate how humbling a concession this was.

The public appreciated the change. Customers noticed an improvement in service and overall disposition towards them. They began to choose underground transit again. The Metro has enjoyed success ever since.

While decades have passed since this case study, human nature has not changed. Not unlike human nature, it's in the nature of company leadership to be motivated by self-preservation. It's human nature to focus on and talk about ourselves.

Remember that Zoom call when you spent most of the meeting looking at your video feed and not the other people in the meeting? While we tend to focus on ourselves, it's customer nature to want the focus to be on them.

Keeping customers at the core results in three benefits that are certain to grow your business with today's consumers.

The Benefits Of Prioritizing Service

When you keep your customers at the core, you can expect clear marketing, improved customer experience, and better referrals.

Let's look at all three and why they are so critical today.

1. CLEAR MARKETING

Today's consumer is inundated with marketing messages and will instantly disregard any message that is not relevant to a problem they are trying to solve.

You have to get specific to be effective. In its early days, lululemon had a hard time getting the attention of the yoga community.

To solve this, they leased space in the heart of Vancouver's yoga community. They advertised yoga classes right in the middle of the store. When the course was over, they brought out all the clothes for everyone to see.

> Consumers bombarded by marketing messages have adapted by tuning out anything irrelevant.

According to Chip Wilson, that's when the company's brand started to take off. They knew whom they were targeting and could create clear, effective marketing.

When you are clear on who your Who is, you can stop wasting

time and money on marketing that doesn't work. The best way to be effective in your marketing is to clarify with whom you are talking.

Having a clear Who gives you a story that creates a consistent story to tell in your marketing. It's the story of your Who's problem, the solution you offer them, and clear visualization of the transformation your Who will experience when working with you.

It's time to stop being guilty of "random acts of marketing." To avoid wasting time and money, your marketing needs to be clear. There is nothing clearer than knowing whom you are talking to and then speaking directly to them.

Why People Ignore Us

Lee LeFever wrote in his book *The Art of Explanation* about a condition that could be affecting you without your even knowing about it. This ailment especially affects anyone who is good at what they do. LeFever calls this condition "The Curse of Knowledge."[4]

I'll explain the leading symptom of the curse of knowledge. Even though you think and talk at the highest levels of your industry, you have a hard time communicating what you do to others in a way they can understand.

You are at risk of possessing the curse of knowledge when your expertise in your industry is higher than anyone outside of it. The consequence comes when you explain what you do. You're attempting to explain it to someone who does not possess the same level of technical or intellectual understanding as you.

When I first started working with chiropractors, I was the third wheel in many conversations. I had no idea what they were talking about most of the time. There was much jargon thrown around. While I pretended to know some of it, most was nonsense to me. And when I talked about marketing and all the latest tech tools, I had to learn how to explain new concepts in a way that they could grasp. They were great at helping people feel better by solving musculoskeletal problems. They weren't great marketers.

And that's ok. You can't do it all.

If a chiropractor asks me how they can get more patients, I couldn't just say, "You need to maximize your funnel to get a better ROAS. By cleaning up your CTA, we can add 20% of your top-line revenue and grow your CTR."

The message, while accurate and insightful, will not get through to them. That's the curse of knowledge doing its thing.

You miss opportunities when you try to sound smart and talk over people's heads.

People who suffer from the curse of knowledge miss partnership opportunities because they talk way over others' heads. They fail to make critical connections with the very people they need to work with.

Businesses that are motivated by helping people know that the goal of communication is not to look important or intelligent.

The purpose of communicating with others is to impart some knowledge to them that will *help them*. A communicator is a bridge builder. The communicator starts the bridge where the recipient is at, not where they should be.

To do this, you need to meet them where they are at, not where you want them to be. We now need to look at what's going on in someone's brain when you're trying to get a message across to them.

Understand and apply this, and your connections with others will skyrocket.

Adapted To Tune Stuff Out

I want to introduce you to a part of your brain that has both helped you and hindered you throughout your life. It's called the "Reticular Activating System," or RAS. You'll find it at the base of your brain, near the top of your neck.

It's the part of our brain that filters out the noise, useless information, and other senses that are jockeying for position into our consciousness. At any given moment, there are millions of stimuli that you could choose to focus on. Our brains can only process so much at a time.[5]

The RAS is the part of the brain that helps you notice the other cars on the road just like yours. You never noticed them until you were driving in one. Then you saw them everywhere. What was happening? Did those cars even exist before you bought one? Of course, they did. Your RAS didn't think it was important to you. Then it did. Now you see them all the time.

Our RAS has its preferences. It wants to feed us a steady supply of new, engaging, and relevant information. Thankfully, there's a way around these strident gatekeepers of our consciousness.

When you Start With Who, you know what is new, engaging, and relevant to those you are trying to reach. When you are clear with your Who, you can catch their attention with what you know is essential to them.

If you can do this, it wakes people out of their adapted daydreaming. It gets through the RAS, so you have a window to speak to them.

If you want clear marketing that connects and gets you the best return, don't try to reach everyone. Focus on the Whos that you can help and speak to your people right where they are. Clear marketing is the first advantage of putting customers first.

2. AMAZING CUSTOMER EXPERIENCES

Think of the best experience you've had that involved another business.

It could be a memorable meal you had with a date or friends. It could be a service you received when you hired another vendor. It could be anything.

If you had a fantastic experience somewhere, I guarantee that it was not accidental. The pleasant experience was a mix of someone's time, energy, and leadership in making it happen.

If you had a bad experience, you could audit the company and trace the negligence back somewhere. A bad experience is the fruit of values, policies or procedures that did not put the customer's needs first.

As mentioned, Amazon exists to serve its customers first. From the time it was a small startup running out of Jeff Bezos' Seattle garage to the day it became the top online retail company globally, Amazon has always been guided by its commitment to its customers first.

The mission and vision of Amazon.com are well known and worth sharing again:

 Our vision is to be Earth's most customer-centric company; to build a place where people can come to find and discover anything they might want to buy online.[6]

Amazon has flourished because it started with Who and never wavered from its commitment. From day one, it's been creating outstanding service for its customers.

Noteworthy success like we've seen with Amazon doesn't come by accident. Jeff Bezos was initially ridiculed for putting an empty chair in every meeting at Amazon. While it was an awkward use of meeting space, Bezos did it to remind everyone that the customer experience had to be at the heart of every decision Amazon made. What seemed weird at the time, we consider genius now.

Start With Who companies are customer-centric. That means they put the customer at the forefront of the company. Because Amazon makes every decision with the customer experience in mind, they ensure outstanding experiences. Companies like this are thriving today and show the promise of a bright future.

What Customer Experience Is All About

The best way to define customer experience is how the customer feels about your company throughout their journey with you. Your customer's experience includes how they feel about interactions with your people and your products. It spans the entire customer life cycle; from consultation, onboarding, and service, to the time you wrap up the project and ask for a Google Review.

Today's customers hold all the power. Competition in our global economy makes keeping people happy a challenge. It's just as easy for someone to rave about how great you are on social media as it is to tarnish your brand in a post.

Providing excellent customer experiences protects you from getting on the wrong side of the mob of public opinion. One harmful blog, post, press release or review can do immense damage to your company.

Brand loyalty is critical. Happy customers mean repeat business and positive buzz about your company.

What are you doing to create a remarkable customer experience? We literally want your customer's experience to be so dynamic that they cannot help but remark about it with others.

There are some simple steps to improve your customer journey:

- **Make sure your whole team reads this book.** It's no use if you're the only one on your team growing a heart for service. You're not the only one customers are interacting with. Your entire team needs to have a love, passion, and understanding for the people your business exists to serve. They can't be bitter or apathetic about what they must do each day for your customers. Assign the first few chapters of this book to them for essential reading. This is an up sell that's in the best interest of creating outstanding experiences for your customers.

- **Think through your processes and how people go through the customer journey.** What's it like to be on the other side of your business? Do customers always know what the next step is? If not, their confusion will lead to frustration. When people don't know what to do, they can become discontented and may leave and move on to your competition. Is your onboarding clear and straightforward? Do they always know what is coming next in the process of working with you? Consider your communication with customers and how you lay out the plan that ends in their success.

- **Have a great website that speaks to them.** When you design your site, don't create it thinking about what *you* want it to include. Think about what a first time visitor needs to see. Is the messaging on your website clear to your Who? Is the language simple enough to accommodate their scanning of your services? Is there enough content there for those who want to research what you do? Finally, do browsers know what you can do for them and what they should do to get help?

If your customer experience is not exceptional, you are at risk of being trashed online and replaced by another company motivated to serve the customer's first.

Whether you like Amazon's success or not, it's hard to deny that customer service prioritization has left its competitors on the scrap heap of business history.

> The power today belongs to the consumer. One bad review can turn away new leads and keep you up at night for weeks.

What are your customers experiencing when they work with you? Are they underwhelmed, overwhelmed or just whelmed?

Suppose clear marketing and excellent customer service are two benefits of prioritization. In that case, the third is about leveraging those to get a boost in future business through the ever-sought after referral.

3. BETTER REFERRALS

Companies that prioritize serving their customers create happy customers. Happy customers can quickly become raving fans who voluntarily tell their peers and colleagues (your other Whos) about how awesome you are. That's the dream. You get to work with the customers you love and then clone them over and over.

Think about your Who and what kind of experience they expect to have to interact with your brand. In his book *Talk Triggers*, Jay Baer points out that the secret to a positive customer experience, the kind your Whos love to talk about, is exceeding a customer's expectations. The more you exceed what they thought they were getting, the more likely they will speak of you with a friend.

Baer wisely points out that most of your best customers come from referrals from your other best customers. If that's the case, why do most business owners and marketers have no strategy for generating more referrals?

According to a *HubSpot* blog:

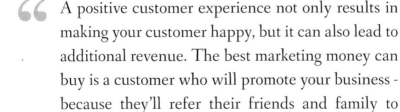 A positive customer experience not only results in making your customer happy, but it can also lead to additional revenue. The best marketing money can buy is a customer who will promote your business - because they'll refer their friends and family to you, free of charge. [7]

To get better referrals, exceed your current customers' expectations.

Always over-deliver with value. You get the best reaction from customers when they get more than they thought. Your customers want to be impressed. They subconsciously expect the *status quo* but, deep down, they want to be wowed.

Commenting on the explosive growth of Facebook, company Founder and CEO Mark Zuckerberg once told the NY Times, "People influence people. Nothing influences people more than a recommendation from a trusted friend."[8] Are your customers telling their friends about you? How do you set up your business, so that's happening all the time?

Exceptional and unexpected customer experiences creates raving fans.

Seek to provide a customer experience that people will discuss at coffee shops, around water coolers, on social media, at the dinner table, and anywhere else they go.

When you know your Who, you can work hard to provide unforgettable experiences for them that they will love to talk about.

Get on the Cutting Edge in Business Today

Imagine how great it would feel if the three common challenges (marketing, customer experience, and referrals) facing 21st-century businesses today could be solved for you.

What if you had an industry-leading ROI for your marketing, outstanding customer experiences, and you were welcoming warm leads all the time. How great would it be if you knew every marketing dollar was an investment with a great return? What if you knew that each day your company was creating remarkable customer experiences that wowed people? And what if those experiences led to a steady stream of referrals?

My friend, this is like business leader heaven we are describing.

It can happen. But it all starts with how you feel about people.

It won't happen by focusing on fulfilling your own needs.

It won't happen by obsessively chasing the competition.

It will happen when you put the customer's flourishing as the driver of your business. Your marketing gets clearer, your customer experiences will improve, and that will lead to rock-star referrals.

That's why effective, growing companies Start With Who.

---

1. Wilson, Chip. *Little Black Stretchy Pants: The Unauthorized Story Of Lululemon*. Self Published, Vancouver, BC. 2019.
2. See CNBC article: "Jeff Bezos: When you find a business opportunity with these traits, 'don't just swipe right, get married'" Published Sept. 14, 2018. https://www.cnbc.com/2018/09/13/amazon-jeff-bezos-4-traits-a-good-business-opportunity-should-have.html
3. O'Reilly Terry. *This I Know: Marketing Lessons From Under The Influence*. Published by Knopf Canada (2017).
4. LeFever, Lee. The Art of Explanation

5. For more information read this fascinating article "Reticular Activating System" https://www.sciencedirect.com/topics/neuroscience/reticular-activating-system Accessed April 10, 2021

6. Taken from their HR website: amazon.jobs

7. https://blog.hubspot.com/service/what-is-customer-experience

8. "Facebook is marketing your brand preferences (with your permission)" NY Times, Nov 7, 2007. https://www.nytimes.com/2007/11/07/technology/07iht-07adco.8230630.html

EIGHT

How You Grow A Thriving Business By Serving A Niche

 Look after people, and people look after you.

– Sam Walton

Now that you're getting clarity on the importance of prioritizing people in your business, let's finish by clearly defining your Who. Once we have that, we can create a plan to effectively reach them.

This 3-step framework will guide your business from concept to product and will be a major contributor to your sales and marketing efforts.

The Who, What, How Framework

Here is a summary of each step:

1. ***Start With Who.*** This is where you get clear on your target audience, customer avatar, ideal client, or the tribe you desire to help and serve. During this step, you will break down the demographics, desires, and decisions of your Who.

2. ***Clarify Your What.*** This is when you develop your product, service, course, or whatever you want to solve your Who's problem.

3. ***Leverage The How.*** The How identifies, implements, and executes what tools you will use to reach your people. The tools you select will be the ones that, when combined, will be the most effective in reaching your Who.

Let's go through each of these steps in greater detail. We will consider some practical suggestions for developing your brand so that it's always close to the heart of your Who.

1. Start With Who

Getting this foundation step is critical. If you fail to get specific about your ideal customer at first, you will pay for it for the duration of your business. Everything will become more complicated.

- Your marketing will be diluted because you won't be able to speak directly to an avatar
- Your sales strategy will suffer because you won't know who or where to target your efforts
- You processes will suffer because you won't be able to automate your steps since you're reinventing the wheel so often
- You will feel spread thin as an organization without being able to specialize

Let's make sure that doesn't happen. Who would you say is your Who?

I'm sure that throughout this book, you've been putting together some ideas about your Who. It's time to focus your thoughts and get the clarity you need to start targeting these people in your business.

Here's the question to guide your thinking. Ask yourself:

"Who are we/am I passionate about helping win their story?"

You want to start a business because it will help someone. You want to be a part of making their lives a little better. Remember, if there are no people involved at the other end, you've only got a hobby. Hobbies are fun, but they do not pay the bills.

Think about the most significant problem you solve for other people. There are many problems to choose from. In our broken world, we are all confronted with problems every day.

Everyone deals with some form of struggles in their lives: health, marriage, their kids, losing money, wasting time, bad habits, slow technology.

Even when we solve some problems, more problems open up. If I lose twenty pounds, that's a problem solved - great! My new problem is that my pants and shirts don't look right anymore. If a business is growing - that's a fun problem to have. The problem becomes that a growing business will face a new set of challenges caused by the chaos of growth.

We cannot get away from problems. Dealing with problems we cannot solve on our own is frustrating at best and debilitating at worst.

The good news is that this world is also full of problem solvers. We can all help make someone's life a little better by solving one or some of their problems. You don't have to solve all of them, just one or two to start. You will help make life better by helping them overcome something that's hindering them. Or, your solution may also be preventative and help them avoid a problem that could occur.

We must stay in contact with our Whos. "Contact" in this case means continually keeping tabs on what problems people in your market are facing. This could mean picking up the phone and making calls. It could also mean joining groups on social media and observing the conversations that are happening.

If you don't check in from time to time on your customers' pulse, your company will lose the heartbeat of the market. You'll put your company at risk of creating something brilliant that nobody needs or wants.

Make someone's life a little better by solving a problem for them.

By keeping close to your Who, you can test to see if there's an appetite for your ideas. People with problems create markets. Successful companies seize those opportunities because it's in their DNA to help people. By helping people, they get rewarded financially and can enjoy the continued growth of their brand.

Fighting The Fear And Being Ok With Saying "No"

Saying "Yes" to your Who means you must also say "No" to many other people as a result.

When you fall in love with someone, you are excited to see them. They walk into a room, and you say "Yes!" inside. Their name shows up on your phone, and you feel an astounding "Yes" again. As the relationship develops, commitment to each other grows. Each day you exclaim "Yes" to that someone who now knows you, loves you, and even tolerates your quirks.

The progression of a relationship means you say more "Yeses" to this person. Still, you always are saying "No" to others.

Finding your Who means you get the joy of saying "Yes" to a particular type of customer. When done right, commitment is powerful. It's scary, sure, but it's the way to go if you want to make income and impact.

I am well aware of the fear of saying "No" to potential customers (or a whole vertical full of them). As my business has grown and evolved, my team and I have often learned to say "No" to projects outside our target market. It's not that we don't want the business. It's just that we have honed our offers to focus on the Whos we have identified and wish to serve more effectively. The more you focus on your Who, the less time you'll have for any other niches. The good news is the risk of saying "No" is always worth it.

Instead of being scary (like most people initially feel about cutting some customers out of their revenue), it is incredibly liberating.

Experience, along with trial and error, has taught us why it's crucial to niche. Without a niche, we had to work with customers we knew nothing about. Since we were not experts in their industry, we made mistakes and experimented on tactics that didn't work. These costly lessons created skepticism with clients. Going forward, they were (understandably) wary of accepting our suggestions. They would then criticize our work, making it almost impossible to deliver a solution that represented our excellence standard. It took us more time to learn a new industry (thus cutting profits).

Today, we accept the fact that we can't help everyone. It's wonderfully liberating.

Freeing ourselves from other niches allows us to be more committed to our Who.

Without a niche, you'll work harder and longer for customers you know nothing about.

When you are committed to your Who, you are free from the thought of having to please everyone else. To niche or not to niche? That's a good question. I say, "niche."

In Western culture, a couple will date each other for a while to determine if they are a good fit. By spending time together, the two become closer, and the commitment to each other goes deeper.

Simultaneously, the trust for each other grows. As a couple visualizes a future together, they make the ultimate commitment of marriage. I'm not telling you to go all-in with your Who until you have dated for a while. I am suggesting that you look for deeper feelings and connections to determine if the next step is worth saying "No" to everyone else.

Is it that vital and worth the effort of narrowing down your Who? If you're on the fence at all, let me ask this:

If you could have *more* of your best customers and *fewer* of the ones you know are trouble (and continue to be a thorn in your side), wouldn't you want to test narrowing down your Who?

It seems like a no-brainer to me.

Who Do You Love To Help?

You likely have some idea about whom you feel you can help the most. These are the ones you enjoy serving (you don't want to work with people you can help but don't like). The days don't feel like drudgery. They say, "Thank you for your tireless help and expertise." You don't even feel like it was anything heroic at all. Helping them may have even been fun at times.

Here are some questions that will get you started on identifying and getting clarity on your Who:

Who are your favorite people to help?

- *What's the coolest outcome you've achieved for someone?*
- *Who are your best success stories?*
- *Who do you like working with?*
- *Who gives you the most money to do it?*

Once you answer these questions, look for the common denominator. Does a particular demographic, industry, personality, or type of company keep coming up?

Write down the Who that you think you're leaning towards. Don't worry about getting this perfect. It's totally fine to write your Who in pencil for now. As it becomes clearer, you can use permanent ink or even a sharpie to solidify your choice.

Once you have a general idea of who your *Who* is, the next step is to clarify *what* you can do for them. Don't rush ahead until you do this. The second point won't work until you have a clear Who in mind.

---

2. Clarify The What

It's time to move to your offer. What will you do to help your Whos?

These people want to get somewhere in their lives. The problem is that as it stands right now, they can't.

They are stuck at A. They need to get to B. The good news is that you and your company are set up to help people get from A to B.

That's what you do every day. Transforming lives is all you do.

There are many different kinds of What you can offer. You can be a professional matchmaker, offer spiritual development courses, invent a health product. I've even heard of a guy who makes $1 million a year teaching people how to do handstands properly.

Let's look at some ways you can create solutions to solve your Who's problems:

Invent A Product

All those little gadgets you have around your house or the office were the brainchild of someone who saw a need in the market and filled it. You could do that too. What's stopping you from designing the next product that meets a need.

A while ago, someone saw something poorly done, and it triggered them. They slammed the table and said, "There must be a better way." Then the product emerged. The product is going to be what solves a problem, satisfying a need in the market.

Provide A Service

When we're stuck, we look to someone who can get us unstuck. When we need help, there's always a service out there that will be willing to bail us out.

While my kids are young, I confess that I don't do much around my house due to the stuff that plagues most homeowners. When I'm not working, I want to be around my wife and kids.

So I hire out my lawn maintenance, house cleaning, gutter cleaning, house washing, and even Christmas light installation. My wife and I are not among the elite in terms of wealth, but we know when it's best to hire someone to carry out a service for us.

People who do services well are incredible human beings. They make my life run smoother. They make me a better husband and father. I'm always grateful for these people.

Is there anything you can do to help people like me? I have many needs outside of my own home. I need marketing help, sales help, content-generating help, I need operations help, scaling help, automation help, software/IT help...the list goes on and on.

Thankfully, someone out there is offering a service for these needs.

You could offer services as a consultant, mentor, leader of a MasterMind group, or anything that better equips your Who in some way. Whatever you do that helps them overcome the barriers holding them back from becoming the people they want to be.

Remember, if enough people are struggling with something, you know you've got a market there.

How you scale them to make an even more significant impact - well, that's beyond the scope of this little section. The good news is there's someone out there offering a service to help achieve it.

Teach A Course

People need your expertise. There are things you know that others would benefit from learning, as well.

The good news is that now you can reach anybody, anywhere around the world, and impart to them your knowledge.

The Internet has completely disrupted the education space. More than ever, people are hungry to learn. Learning used to happen only from conventional places like universities or schools. Education is a billion-dollar industry now. Technology has democratized how we do education. Today you can access any expert in the world from whom you want to learn. You don't have to be in the same room anymore. You can learn from them wherever you are.

It's a wonderful time in history to be an educator.

If there is something you know that could help your Who, outline the process from start to finish. List each step to get from where they are to where they want to be. That's what you will sell: The journey to get where they want to go. Now design a course that will take your Whos along the path.

Create A Widget

Every app on your phone that helps your life was once just an idea from someone who thought they could make another life better. While some may argue that technology and widgets are not improving anyone's life, I disagree. I can tell you many people are healthier, wealthier, more organized, better connected, and getting more business because someone designed a widget for their situation.

What Will You Offer?

The above are just a few options for delivering a What to your Who.

Remember that products, services, courses, widgets, and anything else you create must solve a problem for your Who. If you are not solving a problem, you are wasting time on something that history will prove to be another bad idea.

Whatever you do, you need to show that it is valuable and worthy of your customer's time and money. If it solves a problem, people will pay for it.

> You must show that your offer is valuable and worthy of your customer's time and money.

It's your job to cast a vision for their lives after they take your offer. Transformation sells. You have to put on your sales hat and paint a picture with your words about what they expect their lives to be like on the other side.

When you do that well, you'll get the sale. The value is in the transformation. That's what you're selling.

Does Your Idea Pass The Credit Card Test?

Here's a practical piece of advice I received that could save you years of your time and thousands of dollars.

Before you make anything (the service, the course, the widget, etc.), see if someone will buy it. Don't create it until someone hands you their credit card to (at least) reserve it. This offer of their credit card represents their commitment to accept what you're offering to do.

If you can't sell it once (or ten times is better), you haven't tapped into a pain point well enough and you need to reconsider if you have the right What.

If your offer fails the test, you may have a sales problem. Worse than that, you may have to start again and go back to the drawing board on your offer.

Selling an idea before you create it could be the best advice you'll find in this book. It's going to save some people years of their life because they never followed through on launching the wrong thing. It could be a powerful idea but if there is no market for it, you'll be wasting time. Not spending your time on the wrong idea will open up some capital to invest in the good ideas you'll create.

Secure that first dollar and the others will follow.

Knowing Your Value And How Much To Charge

There must be something about living on the West coast that spurs entrepreneurial innovation. In a previous chapter, I shared the story of Chip Wilson and the explosive growth of lululemon. This is the lesser-known Vancouver-based entrepreneurial story that gets a little weird.

Canadian Douglas Bevans made the news in 2018 selling bottled water for $40 (per bottle!). What was the secret ingredient that made his water such a luxury?

It was no secret at all. We will all recognize it and kick ourselves for not thinking of selling it as well. This luxury $40 water is composed of the excess water remaining in the pot after boiling wieners.

It sounds like a joke, and maybe it is. The profits were no joke, however. Bevans, the inventor of the product, purposed to make a statement about just how gullible people are to gain any health advantage. He claimed that the nutrients collected from the water leftover from boiling hot dogs had terrific health benefits.

While many people laughed, he said others were impressed by the health benefits they'd experienced with his unique products.

To create a buzz, Bevans attended trade shows wherever he could. He gained a following. These customers believed in his claim about the benefits of hot dog water. And so was born another addition to the flooded nutraceutical industry.

"How is this weiner water selling?" you might be wondering.

According to Bevans, it has done very well.

This product's whole point was not to create a health craze but to demonstrate how readily people accept a message even if it has zero credibility.

Douglas Bevans discovered a market created by people who wanted to improve their brain function and made a product they thought would help them.

Before you judge, do a Google search on the health benefits of placebos. It's most certainly a thing.

While I do not endorse deception, Bevans knew that the water industry was full of people who would be willing to pay way too much money for a product that they thought could help them get the edge.[1] Pricing a product is all about the value in the eyes of the consumer. It's your job to find out how much your Whos value what you offer.

If That's How Much Water Can Go For, How Much Can You Charge?

Most entrepreneurs have no idea how much they should be charging.

This is the glaring challenge we face as entrepreneurs: *how much do we charge?*

Let me tell you about a product that I think could charge a lot more for what they sold me. Mind you, I didn't always feel this way.

Young parents know that having a baby is a beautiful gift. It's also a gift that comes with a hefty price tag. You have to sacrifice a lot when you get one. Not many other gifts demand so much from the person receiving them. Of course, with three of these gifts at home, I wouldn't trade them for anything.

When we had our first child, Hayley and I found ourselves making many trips to the store to get another "just one more thing." As new parents, we wanted to make sure we were well prepared.

Those thirty dollar "just one more things" added up. The act of nesting was bleeding our bank account with a bunch of thirty-dollar paper cuts.

Wise counsel advised us to make sure we picked up a product called a "Diaper Genie." Even those without kids can still guess the function of this product: It collects diapers. Rather than a traditional open-ended garbage can, the Diaper Genie contains a diaper and traps everything, most notably, the smell.

When I saw the price tag on an item whose sole purpose was to collect diapers, I cried, "Halt." Why would we need to spend $35 on another garbage can? We had garbage cans in a variety of styles and colors positioned all over the house. We did not need another.

Or so I thought.

I was telling my friend, who also had babies at home, about my plight. He strongly insisted that we go ahead and purchase the "Diaper Genie." His firm exhortation convinced me to buy the plastic diaper-holding tower for $35. I surrendered my hard-earned money and was upsold on some expensive replacement bags that came as an option (but are still essential for the product to be operational).

Though I was reluctant at first, it didn't take long until I started to see the value of this purchase. I noticed the power of the Diaper Genie when we didn't use it. Dirty diapers began to collect in the regular garbage cans scattered about the house. Within an hour, our house smelled like someone parked an outhouse in our living room. After enough of those, I purposed in my heart that the Morrison family would be committed to always using the Diaper Genie.

If we needed more replacement bags, I'd happily pay.

When it was time to get more, the bags' price was utterly irrelevant. I would have been willing to pay twice as much.

I saw the power of perceived value in action. Before kids, I thought a diaper holder wasn't worth $35. Now it's a bargain.

Some people think a Starbucks coffee isn't worth $5.00 since it's got about $0.35 of product in it. Some people happily pay it every day for their coffee experience. Maybe it's how they feel when going into the cafe or being recognized by their favorite barista. $5 could cover the feel of a warm drink in their hands or the rush they get when the caffeine enters their system. It could cost them $5 for the status that comes from having a green mermaid on your cup. Why do they do this?

It's something they value.

A "What" must be something of value for our Whos. How valuable it is can change from person to person. Some people wouldn't pay for a diaper genie when they have garbage cans around.

Some people won't pay more than $1.25 for a cup of coffee. But others will. Those people are Starbucks' Who.

To effectively price like this, your marketing team's responsibility is to build a bridge in your customers' minds between where they are at and who they want to be.

You have to sell the story of their transformation.

Getting them to where they've always wanted to go is worth something to them. What's that worth? Test your market by talking to people. You'll soon figure out what your Who will pay.

From my experience, the number you're thinking of charging is likely too low. You'd probably be fine adding another 15-20%, and your customers would still find it valuable to them.

In summary, every Who needs a What. Getting your What the attention it deserves is a real challenge. That's why it's not enough to have a dynamic product. It would be best if you marketed it. Next, we will figure out some principles in *How* to do just that.

Before moving on, take a moment to define your best What. This is where you start creating that product, service, widget, course, or whatever it is your offering to solve a problem for your Who.

3. Leverage The How

With your ideal client and solution in place, it's time to determine the best strategy to get it to market.

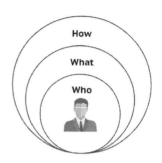

It's easy to become overwhelmed when you consider all the software tools available to market your business.

I don't blame you for not knowing where to begin and then giving up before you start. With so many platforms promising to exponentially increase our revenues, increase productivity, and find better prospects. It's easy to fall victim to "shiny object syndrome," buy everything and use none of it.

Every year at the MarTech Conference (a three-day play date for marketing geeks), marketing guru Scott Brinker awes the crowd by revealing his stats in a presentation called *The Marketing Technology Landscape.*[2] Each year the infographic shocks Brinker's audience (you'd think they wouldn't be so shocked because he does it every year). The visual is presented of all the different software companies out there. Each year, jaws hit the floor as he reveals all the new marketing tools that sprung up in the previous year.

In 2018 there were 6,829 different software tools for marketing.

How many have you tried?

Consider this: In 2011, Brinker counted just over 150 software options to show the growth curve. The number has averaged around 100% growth every year. Every day, new technologies emerge, trying to gobble up market share. They arrest our curiosities as we wonder, "Is this the secret platform I've been looking for all this time?"

I know there are some fantastic products available. Here's a word of caution to anyone like me who wish to chase every shiny new marketing tool that pops up in their newsfeed: All these 6,829 subscriptions we could pay for are *just tools*.

The only comforting thing about chasing these tools is that you get a rush of dopamine released into your body when you purchase a new one. There's a momentary adrenaline rush. For a moment, you think, "This is the tool that's going to take my business to the next level."

This rush, however, is usually short-lived. It's not unlike the feeling of doing drugs. Before long, the thrill fades, and you end up searching for the next "new thing" that will replace the hope and excitement of the last "new thing."

Are you addicted to chasing new tools?

Have you ever found yourself:

- Feeling lost as you look to begin a new business, wondering, "Where do I start?"
- Paralyzed by all the options you can use to optimize sales and marketing?
- Overwhelmed at the thought of having to learn

another new piece of software?

- Wondering if the new software will be a total waste of time and money?

If you answered "Yes" to any of these questions, this is the ideal chapter for you. By the end of this chapter, you'll have a clear roadmap for the journey ahead of you. The tools will be there. We have to do some work before you get there.

This chapter is about answering the question, "How can I develop my business around the main thing: serving my Who?"

You'll find it a much more strategic and effective alternative to wasting time and money chasing new tools.

Where Your Whos Like To Gather

Once you have an idea of whom you would like to help, it's good to figure out where they want to gather. We talked about hunting already, so here's a fishing analogy, much like it.

When you go fishing, you have a fish in mind that you would like to catch. That fish is usually located in specific areas of the body of water you are fishing in. And that fish usually requires a particular lure or bait to catch it with.

Well, you are going "fishing" for new clients. Once you define the clients you want, you need to go to the right "fishing hole" to find them, and you need to use the right "lure" to catch them.

- *Where do they gather?*

- *Where is their attention?*
- *What will I need to do in order to focus their attention on how I can help them?*

One of the things we know is that people like to congregate.

Human beings like to form groups. We do this in person and online. We've all been doing that since our days on the playground. We did it all through high school, and we've taken it into our adult working lives. We love to be part of something. We dread being alone.

Put a bunch of strangers in a big room, and eventually, they will form groups. I will give you some examples of where you can find your Who and how to engage once you identify them.

How To Find Your Whos

It's time to look at some of the places you can start to look for your Whos. Here are some ideas you can try to make those important connections.

1. SHOW UP AT EVENTS

Something was lost when we shut down in-person events in 2020 and 2021. I'm not sure about your experience but there is a part of me that comes alive when my Whos are around. I didn't realize how special it was to be with people who inspired me like that until it was gone. There's something about a

"Happy Hour on Zoom" that couldn't replicate the feeling. No matter how event planners promote this part of a virtual conference, adding a Zoom happy hour was still just a bunch of people on their computers, drinking alone. It's not the same as an in-person event.

COVID and all the lockdowns and cancellations reminded us of how amazing it is to gather together.

While we used to take it for granted, we now see that it's a privilege to get out of the house and show up to places where you know people like you are gathering.

Where do your Whos hang out? In cities all across the country, networking events take place, packed with people that share common interests. You can find conferences on virtually every topic. Now you can find virtual conferences on any subject as well.

You can determine which events are suitable for your target market. You'll know which events create the best fruit for you and how you should engage them. Maybe you'll be a vendor, lead a breakout session, present a keynote, or show up and walk the halls. Whatever you do, there's nothing better than "showing up" and connecting with people.

I will never forget my first conference where I had my "a-ha" moment. This was when I realized the power of networking at conferences. A friend invited me to a chiropractic conference in Las Vegas. The conference didn't thrill me, but the location was appealing. I'm not a chiropractor, so that was a bit of a barrier. I had to get over this and step out of my comfort zone to still engage in their conversation. Eventually, I started to learn the lingo. Something happened during that conference that changed me. I now had memories, shared experiences, and some credibility from chiropractors. I came home exhausted but with numerous leads that converted much better than any cold call or email would ever do. Some of my best clients were the direct result of attending a conference where I met someone and got into a great conversation, which led to a meeting. The meeting led to a big sale. That year I made some substantial relational gains. I was invited into group chats by text, into Facebook groups, and helping plan accommodations for next year's attendees. The following year's conference was different than my first experience. It was a reunion! I honestly didn't even care about the Vegas part because I was so excited to hang out with the people who were now both my clients and friends.

What if you feel like you're too remote and there are no groups around you? Thankfully, we have a fantastic resource available to us that previous generations could never have imagined. Technology allows us to connect without having to be in the same place. What have we done with this ability? We have gotten together into groups (aka "social networks").

Live events are memorable. They provide you with a tremendous, unprecedented opportunity to find your Whos. There's nothing like looking someone in the eye, shaking their hand, and building a relationship.

2. **LEVERAGE THE CONNECTING POWER OF SOCIAL MEDIA**

There are two types of people using social media: There are the takers and the givers. Let me describe the characteristics of both. You can diagnose yourself based on the following descriptions:

A. The Takers

Too many people go on social media intending to consume. They open the phone and try to take something. They mindlessly scroll, looking for something. Sometimes it's to be entertained, informed, or to have their opinions reinforced. Whatever they're looking for, they are there to consume only, just like a leech. Someone else put themselves out there. Someone else wrote the article. Someone else shot the video. They just took it in. That's not how you leverage a How. It doesn't connect you to your Whos.

Some people turn to social media trying to give, but they still end up as takers because it is clear they're just in it to draw attention to themselves. Someone told them that the best way to gain a following or earn a million dollars online is to provide the internet with more content. While they may check all the boxes and show up, it soon becomes clear that they are not showing up to serve.

They're just in it for the clicks, likes and other vanity metrics. Those are the takers. They're the ones giving social media a bad reputation (they're not the only ones creating this lousy reputation. Some could say it's the app designers themselves. That discussion goes outside the scope of this discussion).

Takers use social media as another way to draw attention to themselves.

B. The Givers

The Givers understand that while they may never have a pure motive, they know social media's purpose. Givers understand that social media is a tool to get exposure to their How in serving their Who. For the sake of others, they show up regularly and contribute to the conversation. Sometimes they are on the camera, and they are interacting with the person on the camera. A giver is consistently starting conversations for the sake of helping. They will also engage in further discussions and offer suggestions, help, and feedback. If there is a question, they will take the time to provide a thoughtful answer.

Most importantly, Givers build relationships. That's what social media is all about. That's what staying in business is all about. It's not a coincidence. That's what Starting With Who is all about.

Givers go to social media ready to add value where they can. Takers are just there to leech whatever's in it for them. Are you currently a giver or taker on your social media platforms?

The $1.80 Strategy

I love what Gary Vaynerchuk calls his $1.80 *Social Media Strategy*. Vaynerchuk advises business

Givers leverage social media as opportunity to help and serve.

leaders who want to improve their
social media presence to leave their two cents on discussions across various social platforms. According to Vaynerchuk, you have to give your two cents ninety times a day. That means offering something as simple as a like, an emoji is acceptable. An insightful comment or word of encouragement on a post is even better. These two cents delivered ninety times adds up to $1.80 each day, hence the name $1.80 *Social Media Strategy*. It's takes about an hour each day to do it well.[3]

The small, consistent, incremental marketing investment is compelling.

When you add value in some small way ninety times a day, you start to become known and become a respected voice in the community where you want to establish yourself.

3. GET A WEBSITE THAT CONNECTS WITH YOUR WHOS AND HELPS YOU WIN

Website shame is a real thing. Introducing myself and describing what I do makes people uncomfortable. I saw it for years before whenever I mentioned the words "I'm a pastor." People stared at the ground, shuffled their feet as all kinds of feelings came to them. Telling someone, I was a pastor was the ultimate conversation killer. It was a brilliant card to play when doing introductions on a plane. You should try it. If you ever don't find yourself wanting to talk to someone on a flight, just tell them you're part of the clergy. They won't bother you for the rest of the flight!

Today, I get the same reaction when I tell business leaders that I do websites. They look down. They shuffle their feet. All kinds of emotions come up. It's mostly shame, I can tell. They are not proud of the way they have managed their company's web presence. In fact, their website embarrasses them. They stopped pointing people to it years ago.

That's a missed opportunity. It's years of missed opportunities depending on how long it has been like that.

Fixing up a website is beyond the scope of this book. As it relates to Starting With Who, I will say this: *One of the reasons why websites perform poorly is because they are company-centric and not Who-centric.*

Websites that are not doing well are usually the result of having no guidance in creating it. Pages and text were put up because it felt right or looked like a competitors.

Here are the questions every company should ask before creating a website to represent their brand:

- Is this something our Whos will find interesting?
- What is the problem our Who wants to solve?
- Does it cast a vision for what they life will look like when we solve their problem?
- Does this establish trust so that we emerge as the best option for our Who?
- What is the clearest call to action they should take to start working with us?

Develop Regular, Interesting And Compelling, Content On Your Website

Rule number one for putting content on your site is to make sure it brings value to your Who. When you deliver value, you establish your brand as the expert in that field.

Many of us stare at a blinking cursor, wondering what to write. If you're struggling to think of new content, ask your customers and potential customers what they are struggling with. They will let you know what's keeping them up at night (as it concerns your line of work, of course - you're not offering free counseling).

Staying close to their problems means you will know precisely what kind of content to create on your website.

When you provide good content, you are taking steps to develop trust, and eventually, you will win their business.

Content marketing is the creation and sharing of online material (such as videos, blogs, and social media posts) that serve your audience. Content marketers pump out valuable content across all mediums, confident that those who consume today will become customers tomorrow.

This work of creating valuable content is a critical piece of growing credibility with your Who.

It's about developing trust. All business is built on the foundation of trust. When you help people in their time of need with a piece of content, they learn to trust you.

This hard work of creating valuable content is how you develop credibility with your Who.

Does Your Website Help You Reach Your Who?

Whether they get slowed down by confusing website software or are held hostage by their developer, most businesses don't even bother keeping their website updated. It's too complicated to make changes. The platform they're using doesn't offer anything but problems. When that happens, they give up creating content on their site. The result of that is the site gets ignored and goes a little more out of date every day.

Wouldn't it be nice if you could make a quick change to your site without having to speak geek or attempt to have your developer make the changes before the end of the day?

The technology is now available so that anybody can make content for their site.[4]

4. BECOME AN AUTHORITY BY DEVELOPING YOUR SKILL AS A SPEAKER

Notice that the heading isn't called "Public Speaking." That would lead most people to skip this section entirely. I'm advocating instead for "Speaking." It's way different. While even the thought of talking in front of a crowd makes people sweat, the art of speaking is a powerful tool to reach crowds en masse and grow your impact.

Since the time of Greco-Roman culture, the orator has always been an authority figure in our culture. Today, it's the TED and conference speakers who hold enormous power.

You'll be successful connecting with your Whos if you can seize this opportunity. Every entrepreneur and every company needs a signature talk or presentation that you can deliver at any moment.

Being able to share the message of your brand publicly is something every entrepreneur should master. Take every chance to share the solution you offer, even if it is not directed to your Who.

Speaking is a powerful way to reach new crowds, become an authority, and grow your impact.

A powerful talk will be one of your most significant ways to be exposed to new people where you can attract new clients. You need a talk that's your own. Only one for now. It's your message. It's that one thing you need to tell your one kind of person. Find the events you know your Whos will be attending and alert event organizers that you have a signature talk that solves a problem for those in attendance. You'll have to start small, but eventually, you will want to do this talk so well you can give it without notes to a crowd of thousands at a moment's notice – how fun would that be?

5. WRITE A BOOK

There's just something about being a published author that has a certain ring to it. A book gives you the authority in our culture.

Books are the best way to boost your credibility, even if many claim that no one reads books anymore. If you've published a book on a subject that your Who finds interesting, you will have instant respect.

You can even publish it yourself and still have authority. Going through a publisher may get you some street cred, but self-publishing still holds weight. The good news is that you have much more control over the content that gets printed when you self-publish. You can publish a book in months rather than waiting for years to get your work to new audiences.

The book you write will add credibility to your brand, compliment your public speaking, put you in a position of authority in your area of expertise.

There's nothing like a book to gain credibility with your Who. Just make sure it is a book worth reading. That's on you.

6. CREATE A COURSE

"How do I ..." are the most common words typed into Google every day. People are going online to learn. We value education. If you put your finger on the pain point of your Who and offer a solution through a course of some sort, you will gain massive trust with them.

Online courses are one of the fastest-growing industries on the Internet today. In addition to that, some software makes presenting and marketing a course as simple as creating a series of videos with matching PowerPoints. Your course can be as simple as just you talking in front of a camera next to a whiteboard. Alternatively, you can go all out and include corresponding presentations with infographics and all the bells and whistles.

Having an authoritative and compelling talk on your expertise, your book, and an online course will seal the deal as an authority in your niche and industry.

Your online course can be free or paid. The point is to transform your Who from point *A* to *B*. It is an effective way to show that you and your company are there to help your Whos win.

7. START A PAID MEMBERSHIP COMMUNITY

Never in the history of the internet has it been an easier or more opportune time to start an online membership site.

A membership site can be something like Netflix, a local gym, or any network of people paying monthly fees to be a part of something that interests them.

A membership site can be a fantastic way to share your expertise, cultivate a community, and create a nice income for yourself. Memberships are a powerful opportunity to:

- Share your in-depth knowledge on a subject your Whos want to learn about
- Lead conversations that build relationships
- Guide your Whos step-by-step from problem to solution
- Cultivate a community of Whos around a topic or outcome

We cannot go into all the details, but there is a ton of information online about how to start a dynamic online membership community with your Whos. Google "Stuart McLaren" and you'll have enough content to do a deep dive for weeks.

8. HOST A PODCAST

Podcasting continues to grow as an effective way to reach new people and develop existing relationships.

Podcasting gives you a captive audience while people cut the grass, go for a run, or commute to work. If you start a podcast, you can share your ideas, your vision, tell customer satisfaction stories, host exciting conversations, or whatever else you can do to add value to the lives of your Who.

One of the overlooked benefits of podcasting is connecting with guests. When you invite a thought leader, influencer, or "guru," you can leverage their influence and expertise to serve your audience while being exposed to theirs.

> Podcasting gives you a captive audience while people cut the grass, go for a run, or commute to work.

Starting a podcast is quick, cheap, and you can do it today. Don't let fear of judgment or perfectionism stop you from taking advantage of this exciting medium. People will appreciate it as you grow with them.

The Who, What, And How Of Scaling A Business

It is beneficial to start building a relationship with your Who long before you ever meet them. That's how you scale all this Who business.

Everything I've recommended in this chapter takes work. You'll have to do some writing, some filming, stretch yourself outside of your comfort zone, and be willing to make some mistakes. What's the point again? The point is to engage in an exercise called: *presuasion*.

Presuasion is a word I didn't make up. I assure you it's not a typo. It didn't get past my editor the first two times this manuscript went by him. I insisted that we need to keep it. The problem is that I don't know who coined the phrase, so I am unsure who to give credit to for coming up with it.

Presuasion helps people see that you are the best fit for their business *before you ever meet them.* We have to persuade people on a sales call when we are pitching what we do. Presuasion is warming up your ideal client so much beforehand that they are ready to hand over their credit card to you before they even get on that call.

Not having to do sales calls or plead with people to give you their business – that, to me, is worth all the work alone.

Imagine how great it would feel to be famous to people that matter to you, but you didn't have all the baggage of being a mainstream celebrity?

How would you answer the following:

> **Presuasion** is convincing a potential customer to hire you long before you ever meet them.

- Are you tired of being another nameless, faceless seat-warmer in a crowd?
- Would you like people to recognize you when you walk into a conference?
- Would you like more respect around the office?
- Wouldn't it be great to be able to double your rates because you were in such high demand?
- Wouldn't it be nice to spend less time on sales calls and more time adding value, scaling your business... and doing pretty much anything other than selling?

If you're excited about the idea of the above questions becoming your reality, consider doubling down on this framework. Put the Who, What, and How to to action and see the difference a little focus and strategy makes.

Imagine how great it would feel to have people seeking you, willing to pay top dollar for the privilege of working with you.

Your team is waiting for the day when customers call them and tell them they have read enough of your content to realize you are the best solution for them.

> **What if you could spend less time on sales calls and more time handpicking the best customers?**

Conclusion: Why A Thriving Business Today Requires a Who, What, and How

If you were starting a new company today, this is how you would do it, right? You'd test a market by finding if there are people that needed what you did. Then you would figure out how to solve the problem for them. Then you'd need to do some marketing of your solution, so you'd have to find crowds of people you can help to let them know what you can do for them. And then you'd have to show up where they were.

Who, What, and How. These are the three keys to reaching your Whos. It's not overwhelming, and with a little thought, you can start right away.

---

1. 'Hot Dog Water' seller in Vancouver gets laughs to prove a point. CTV News, See article in https://www.ctvnews.ca/lifestyle/hot-dog-water-seller-in-vancouver-gets-laughs-to-prove-point-1.3984356 June 18, 2018.
2. See https://chiefmartec.com/ for the latest results.
3. Read more about this here: Vaynerchuk, Gary. *THE $1.80 INSTAGRAM STRATEGY TO GROW YOUR BUSINESS OR BRAND.* https://www.garyvaynerchuk.com/instagram-for-business-180-strategy-grow-business-brand/ Accessed February 10, 2021.
4. If you'd like to see what my team and I have been doing to provide businesses with websites that are easy and quick to make changes, check out getclearsites.com.

NINE

It's Time To Serve, Not Fight

 It's easier to love a brand when a brand loves you first.

-Seth Godin

S ociologists tell us that we as a society are more divided than ever. Politics, race, religion, you've seen, heard, and experienced the things that divide us.

The media prey on this because a good fight always sells. It has always been this way. There's something about a battle in the woods in elementary school that will draw a crowd over a healthy exchange of ideas. Fighting is all too common. While I'm no pacifist, we cannot live our lives going from one fight to another.

If you feel like your life is a daily fight against the market, your competitors, or the demons inside of you telling you to give up, you've now had a vision of a better way.

Let's stop fighting everything and start serving some people we know we can help. It's time to make the kind of impact you know you want in your life. The fighting may provide a rush of adrenaline as you struggle to survive. It will leave an uninspiring legacy and a joyless existence getting there.

As we conclude the book, you will see that you can achieve your Why without having to feel like you've had to fight your way to every opportunity. There is another path: It's the path of service your Who.

You Don't Have To Fight Anymore

Allow me to jog your memory to an epic movie from the early 80s, a classic that was one of the finest stories ever to hit the big screen. Of course, I'm talking about *Rambo: First Blood*.

Rambo is the classic American war hero. The Vietnam vet was a highly trained soldier who was notorious for being great on the battlefield. His struggles came when he tried his hand at civilian life. As a former Green Beret, Rambo is misunderstood as a drifter and is arrested. Rambo quickly escapes his captors and is then chased by the crooked authorities. Not knowing whom they are fighting, they cannot capture Rambo, who survived a Vietnam POW camp and is as tough as anyone.

Rambo's mentor and former commanding officer, Colonel Sam Trautman, radios him and lets him know he doesn't have to fight anymore. Rambo insists they drew first blood. Rambo is a soldier. Fighting is all he knows. In his mind, he must continue to fight. Eventually, after escaping a collapsed mine, blowing up a gas station, and destroying a gun store, Rambo reencounters Trautman. "You don't have to fight anymore" is the theme of their talk. This strikes a nerve with the brave hero. Rambo breaks down in tears and surrenders. Instead of fighting, he agrees to a life of serving his community, leading from his strength and bringing good into the world.

What if, like Rambo, you need to stop fighting every day and start serving? Doesn't that sound more life-giving?

What if you found others who need your help and showed up every day ready to serve them? As we've discussed, the money will be there if you do.

Whatever you do, you're in the business of making other lives better. Help them win their story and be amazed how, in turn, they help you win yours.

Instead Of Fighting To Get Your Why, Start Serving Your Who

We have enough fighting in this world. Remember the last election? I don't even need to specify when or where. They're all nasty blood baths.

The nations, the politicians, the world religions, races, and your competitors.

What if:

- the world took the lead from the best businesses?
- we business leaders could teach the world about the power of serving?
- Starting with Who is the key that unlocks the kind of income and impact that your heart desires?

Instead of fighting for every opportunity you can to promote yourself, what if you just started serving the people you know you help best.

When you serve, you win people over. When you win people over, they talk about you. When they talk about you, the good news travels. It results in more followers, more readers, more listeners, more referrals, and more satisfaction in life (and more people at your funeral, but you won't be able to see that yourself).

That's the kind of impact you've always dreamed of making. It all starts with a commitment to service.

The People Who Need You Today

When we get stuck in a rut, we can easily wallow in pity. We lose hours, days, weeks, months and even years wishing our life and business would be different. Focussing on ourself, it's never enough because we were never meant to be satisfied alone. When it is just us, we miss the opportunity to actually get the thing we are looking for: *a real connection with people.*

Business is a wonderful vehicle for creating authentic connections with people.

If you don't get over yourself, nobody wins. You don't. And the people you can help don't either. Without you, your Whos remain stuck in their problems.

They lose hope each day. Their anxiety grows each day. They wonder if there's anyone who can help them.

Suppose you've lived with anxiety, frustration, loneliness, or some other problem you couldn't solve on your own. In that case, you know how easy it is to turn to despair and hopelessness. The world loses its color. Life seems like it has no purpose.

That's what's going on when your business is not around. Your Who is waiting for you and your team today. They're hoping today is the day you get over yourself and get back in the game. The people you can help are sitting there despondent because their problems are not going away on their own. They're praying that somebody like you would show up and help them break free.

Now, imagine how sad it would be if they never met you and your company. What if they did meet you, but you were so busy being a Brad, talking about yourself and how great you are? You would've missed the chance to make that critical first impression.

That would be terrible. But you're not going to do that because today is a new day. You're starting again with Who.

When You're Starting With Who

Now that you're going to Start With Who, it's time to start connecting with the people you can help. You'll start talking about how you understand how frustrating the pain is, the problems you solve, and the outcomes you deliver.

You'll notice strangers start to trust you. They'll gladly hand you their credit card, eager to sign up for your services, course, widget or whatever you do.

That's how you live a life of purpose. It's time to change lives. It's time to start filling up your funeral.

> It's a powerful motivation to go to work each day ready to serve rather than to take.

It's Time to Tell a Better Story

It's time to work hard to change culture perception in business. What if you and I, by the way we treat our clients, could be a force for changing how our culture sees business? It's time to restore the heart of business. It's about people serving people each day. That's the mindset we approach our work.

My goal in this book in writing *Now Start With Who* has been to serve you as a modern-day "Samwise Gamgee." He's the beloved companion to Frodo in J.R.R. Tolkien's famous Lord of the Rings.

My favorite scene in the book/movie series comes when Frodo is weary from his journey, cannot handle the ring's burden, and wants to give up. He tells his travel companion that he cannot go on anymore.

You may be feeling like you don't want to go on thinking that business is only about growth, making shareholders happy, or just making ends meet. Customers, with that mindset, are just a means to an end. You know it's not satisfying. It just doesn't feel right.

Thankfully, there's a better story to write. Service is a much better story than fighting or exploiting people.

If you feel like you're not enjoying the old way of doing business, let Sam close off the book with his encouragement to Frodo and all of us:

 Sam: I know. It's all wrong. By rights, we shouldn't even be here. But we are. It's like in the great stories, Mr. Frodo. The ones that mattered. Full of darkness and danger, they were. And sometimes you didn't want to know the end. Because how could the end be happy?... A new day will come. And when the sun shines, it will shine the clearer. Those were the stories that stayed with you. That meant something, even if you were too small to understand why. But I think, Mr. Frodo, I do understand. I know now. Folk in those stories had lots of chances of turning back; only they didn't. They kept going. Because they were holding on to something.

Frodo: What are we holding onto, Sam?

Sam: That there's some good in this world, Mr. Frodo ... and it's worth fighting for.

There is a better way. It's about serving. It starts with serving your Who.

Because people are always worth it.

About the Author

Jon is the Lead Consultant at *Get Clear Consulting.* Located on the West Coast of Canada, Get Clear empowers business leaders from all over the world by giving them the tools they need to achieve their goals.

Unlike other agencies that keep you focused on your company, Get Clear helps you develop the mindset and message to transform prospective customers into raving fans of your brand.

As a business leader, husband, and father, Jon knows that true joy and satisfaction only comes when you give up the rights to yourself and pour yourself out in the service to others.

Jon holds an MA from Biola University. He is also an alumnus of Oxford University, a TEDx speaker, and is married to Hayley. They live in Abbotsford, B.C. with their three girls.

For more information about Jon and his team at Get Clear when you visit www.getclear.ca.

Manufactured by Amazon.ca
Bolton, ON

28880378R00129